THE
SALESMAN
WHO
DOESN'T SELL

THE SALESMAN WHO DOESN'T SELL

A MARKETING GUIDE TO MAKING MONEY WHILE YOU SLEEP

BRIAN J. GREENBERG

NEW YORK

LONDON • NASHVILLE • MELBOURNE • VANCOUVER

THE SALESMAN WHO DOESN'T SELL
A MARKETING GUIDE TO MAKING MONEY WHILE YOU SLEEP

Published in New York, New York, by Morgan James Publishing. Morgan James is a trademark of Morgan James, LLC. www.MorganJamesPublishing.com

The Morgan James Speakers Group can bring authors to your live event. For more information or to book an event visit The Morgan James Speakers Group at www.TheMorganJamesSpeakersGroup.com.

ISBN 9781683505976 paperback
ISBN 9781683505983 eBook
Library of Congress Control Number: 2017907931

Cover and Interior Design by:
Chris Treccani
www.3dogcreative.net

In an effort to support local communities, raise awareness and funds, Morgan James Publishing donates a percentage of all book sales for the life of each book to Habitat for Humanity Peninsula and Greater Williamsburg.

Get involved today! Visit
www.MorganJamesBuilds.com

DEDICATION

This book is dedicated to my grandfather, Sam, and my father, Elliott. They have passed down their teachings, and the principles of creating businesses that can run on their own and make money while you sleep.

TABLE OF CONTENTS

FOREWORD

By Marques Colston,
*Former Super Bowl champion wide receiver
for the New Orleans Saints*

As a former NFL champion, I know a lot about contact sports. Digital marketing can be likened to a contact sport. One has to play offense, (aggressive outbound marketing through having a proactive online presence), as well as making sure to have a great defensive lineup, (an effective reputation management). The offense, or aggressive outbound marketing through a strong online presence, scores the points but the defensive team, a proactive online presence, is what wins the championships in sports and life.

I formed Dynasty Digital to help meet the needs entrepreneurs have of both an offensive and defensive marketing playing field. It's the businesses that find the open spots, (differentiate themselves from their competition), who grow the quickest. Strong companies are formed through alliances, strategic partners and a strong team working together to get the message spread widely. No football team has ever lost a game when they scored every time their offense took the field. The field of marketing is very similar. Companies who have mastered the art of marketing and can sell their business every time they are given an opportunity will always experience success.

While no one can manage time, everyone can learn how to properly prioritize it. The defense's job is to get the opponent off the field as quickly as possible in order to give their own offense time to get their job done. While no one can create more time, the most successful companies will learn how to better leverage that time they are given. By building systems and having the right talent in place from the beginning, as well as making sure to have a stellar plan in place with the correct talent/personnel, a company is positioning themselves for the best chance to win.

While scoring on every possession isn't realistic in football or in life, having the right systems in place, such as strong reputation management, cash flow management and a stellar execution will help companies position themselves to be in the best shape possible to leverage their success and keep moving forward. That is what my company does for the companies it works for… and that is why I appreciate Brian Greenberg's approach in this book. Brian takes the topic of marketing, a daunting subject matter in its own right, and breaks it down into manageable, understandable steps. From the entrepreneur just starting out, to the seasoned executive who may have hit a rut, to everyone in between, Brian shows how to use inbound marketing, a group of systems that work on their own to bring organizations business. He provides wonderful information with a straightforward perspective that is easy to understand and implement.

Brian's expertise comes from having run multiple successful companies using the method of inbound marketing, and in the following pages, he'll share his most effective marketing tips—tips that have a proven track record of working. Enjoy.

INTRODUCTION

Let's Look at the World from the Customer's Perspective

"Wah … wa … wa…" (like the teacher in Charlie Brown) is the sound most consumers hear when companies inundate them with conflicting messages about what to eat, watch, wear, and buy. Consumers are overloaded, over-committed, and overdue for a vacation—from telemarketing calls coming in at dinnertime and now even on Sundays, endless e-mail spam, and the postal junk-mail overflowing in our mailboxes. Statistics show that consumers can be bombarded with thousands of sales messages every single day.

Frankly, many of them don't want to be asked to watch, spend, or do one more thing. The demand for their attention and dollars has created a consumer market filled with cynics whose defenses are on full alert. Sales people are hyper-focused on getting to the close, rather than on getting to know the consumer. They fail to realize success requires a relationship that begins and ends with authentic connection.

Customers shouldn't be seen as "audiences" (or as seen in the example of Wells Fargo's telemarketing scandal in 2016, "quotas"). They are neighbors, friends, family members, teammates, co-workers, and citizens.

Salespeople Created this Environment

In a recent Gallup poll, sales professionals were ranked lower on honesty than Congress (ouch)! That may account for why consumers are increasingly looking to their peers, rather than to companies, gurus, thought leaders, or so-called "experts" for advice on what to buy, watch, read, listen to, and eat. Case in point: since Amazon's launch in the late nineties, much of the company's success can be tied to the wealth of opinions available to online shoppers. By hosting millions of consumer reviews, Amazon has become an indispensable resource for consumers from all walks of life.

TripAdvisor, which contains more than 200 million consumer-generated reviews, ranks as the fourth most popular travel site in the United States (out of more than 7,700 sites), with 10.9 million visits per week. This proliferation of user-generated reviews goes to show how consumers' priorities have changed, and how important trusted guidance is to us in deciding how to spend our hard-earned money.

As marketing analytics get more precise, consumers will continue to grow more suspicious, and the companies that will thrive in this environment are the ones whose salesman don't sell!

Why I Wrote this Book

Approximately 2 million books come out each year, thousands of which are business success books. When added to those the thousands of marketing articles that come out annually, it is a ton of information to absorb ... and sadly, most of it is useless. I'm here to help you cut through the clutter. I understand the obstacles that entrepreneurs and business owners face when it comes to marketing their companies. I know because I've been through it all and found a better way—better methods for long-term marketing success.

In this book, I'm going to show you how to build your reputation by leveraging reviews, social media, your website, and all your marketing efforts so you can spur sales without ever having to pick up a phone. I will explain the theory behind inbound marketing—building systems that work on their own to bring people in. I've built three successful businesses utilizing this model, including my flagship company, True Blue Life Insurance. If I stopped marketing today, I'd still attract customers for at least a couple of years because of all the work I've already done.

This is the difference between being an operator and being an owner: An operator's business begins to die the moment he or she stops actively selling, whereas an owner has built a system that isn't reliant on his personal sales efforts day in and day out.

SECTION I

INFLUENCE
WITHOUT SELLING

CHAPTER 1

PERCEPTION BECOMES REALITY: CREATING A PROFESSIONAL BRAND

You are probably familiar with Barbara Corcoran, the New York real estate mogul from *Shark Tank*. She wasn't always a household name, and she wasn't always a mogul. In fact, when she first established her company, she had little experience and less than a handful of brokers. She certainly didn't have any celebrity clients.

That all changed when she took out a few advertisements in which she referred to her company as a consortium of power brokers, claiming they were the best in New York City. Soon after she started calling herself a power broker, other people began referring to her as such. Her claim quickly became reality.

Barbara tells a story about how she landed a television interview in which they asked her about celebrities' real estate-hunting methods, and what the role of the power broker was in assisting them. At the time of the interview, it was unclear whether she'd ever had a single celebrity client. Nevertheless, she answered their inquiries—and immediately following the television show, celebrities began to call her. This is a classic example of perception becoming reality.

Perception

Perception is defined as "a way of regarding, understanding, or interpreting something; a mental impression." Presenting yourself as having already achieved what you want is the first step toward making your dreams a reality.

Every aspect of your personal presentation is an opportunity to shift a buyer's opinion, from the décor of your restaurant to the brand of your shoes. Of course there are businesses that succeed without carefully crafting their image: You may eat at a hole-in-the-wall that is well known for serving the best pad thai in the city. The website Craigslist is notably terrible-looking, but millions of people use it. Still, you don't want to lose customers because you failed to take simple steps to create a positive impression.

It's not only about how you present to other people, but also how you present to yourself. In order for Barbara to have the chutzpah to say, "I am a power broker," she had to believe it could become a reality.

The steps outlined in this book require you to put yourself out there and take action. It can be very difficult to trust your instincts and have the confidence and faith required to succeed. One of the most valuable lessons I can teach you as an entrepreneur is to stop speaking and thinking negatively. I was taught the power of the words "I am" by a great business coach, Peter Winslow. When I stopped following the words "I am" with a negative, it changed my entire mindset.

There is something very powerful about the use of "I am." Any time you say, "I am," pay attention to what follows. Is it, "stupid" or "tired" or "an idiot"? If you are referring to yourself in the negative, catch yourself and stop it. Saying, "I *feel* stupid" is totally different from "I *am* stupid," and worlds away from

"I'm a smart person and intend on not making the same mistake again." Catch how you are perceiving yourself and change it to the positive until it becomes habit.

Once you've begun to improve your self-perception, it's time to turn your attention to how others perceive your business. Sales without selling begins with presenting your company, your product, and even your own personality as professionally as possible. Your job is to address all the questions and concerns a client may have up front, so you don't have to convince him or her later. That's the power of perception.

Creating Your Brand

Your brand should convey all the attributes you want customers to associate with your business. It should create and influence perception.

What follows is a series of eight branding steps that are essential to your success. A few of these steps may seem rudimentary to some readers, but I want to make sure all our bases are covered. Follow these steps, and you'll excel in your industry, stay ahead of your competitors, and reap the benefits of success.

- **Step One: Make It Official**
  You must first incorporate your business as a limited liability company (LLC) or corporation (Inc.). The biggest difference between an entrepreneur and a "want-repreneur" is action. While "want-repreneurs" talk about it, think about it, and even ponder it in the wee hours of the morning, they won't get much further. Entrepreneurs take action.

    Once you're done setting up an LLC or a corporation, you should use your incorporation paperwork and your tax

ID number to open a bank account and get a debit card and a credit card in the business's name.

- **Step Two: Invest in a Well-Designed Company Website**
  In this day and age, if you have a business without a website, people will doubt your legitimacy.

  It's even more important to make sure your website is well designed. People make a lot of excuses for not spending money on their online presence. Most of those excuses are baloney.

  This is not the place to be original. I've heard some people say, "I want to have a great website, but I don't want it to look like everyone else's." This is a huge mistake.

  In business, it's necessary to imitate before you innovate. Don't try to recreate the wheel; emulate the wheel and make it better.

  Start by creating a great logo for your website. Don't make the mistake of designing your website before you've decided on your logo, which establishes a color scheme and personality for your business. You don't have to spend $10,000 to hire a branding firm; it's inexpensive and just as effective to hire a freelancer.

  When I need a logo, I visit websites like Freelancer or 99designs. These websites allow you to hold a contest wherein freelancers compete to create your logo for as little as $250. Holding a $250 contest will yield as many as two hundred different design samples from freelancers all over the world. Request changes and provide input to make your logo perfect. Only after you are completely satisfied do you choose the winner.

The next thing you should do is pick a website platform. I always recommend WordPress, especially for simple websites. If you're creating an e-commerce site, BigCommerce, Shopify, and Magento work well. Use something that's well established—and once again, there's no need to reinvent the wheel.

Go for a premium theme. It will cost between $50 and $250, and it's well worth the price. These can be manipulated to make custom designs—a website like ThemeForest will give you invaluable reviews and insights into which themes to choose. You'll find designs that have been customized and upgraded to look a lot better than the standard template.

Next, hire a designer. I recommend searching Upwork and Freelancer.com, where a professional designer will charge between $500 and $2,500 for a great layout. I don't like working with big agencies because they charge you three times more for the same work. You're paying for their rent and their brand, which is money that could be better spent on *your* rent and *your* brand.

Make sure to use high-quality photographs; do not use free stock images. Spend the money. I go to iStock, Thinkstock, and Shutterstock for high-resolution images that cost between $5 and $35. These images will make your website stand out.

Some people will tell you that you don't need your own website because you can sell your products on sites like Etsy, eBay, or Amazon. The problem is that Etsy and companies like it take a large percentage of the profits. When people do well on sites like these—when they become real businesses—they have to expand beyond the realm of Etsy. Why not make that investment ahead of time?

I suggest selling on these platforms in addition to selling on your own website. Create your logo and start building your brand, because you never know how long these third-party sites will last, or when your big break will require additional resources.

- **Step Three: Hire a Professional Photographer**
Get a professional headshot. Don't let a sloppy photo ruin others' perception of you. These days, a headshot will cost you $150 or less.

  You can easily search for a photographer in your area; Thumbtack is an excellent online resource. Use that headshot on your website, your social-media sites, and maybe even your business card.

  Take it a step further and get professional headshots for your team as well. Your team members can use the photos for their social-media sites, and you can create a team page on your website. Great companies promote their teams on their websites, and you should too.

- **Step Four: Invest in High-Quality Business Cards**
Business cards are often the portal to your professional image. Take it up a notch from services like Vistaprint, which will often leave you with something that is too small and poorly done, and opt for premium business cards on better paper stock.

  I use thick, colored-edge business cards from THikit. com. I opt for 32-point card stock (14-point card stock is the norm) for everyone at my companies.

- **Step Five: Set Up a Cloud-Based Phone System**

  When I started my first e-commerce business, there were only two of us: my father and me. But I had a toll-free number through a company called RingCentral that provided unlimited extensions for $25 per month. When people called, they heard, "Thanks for calling Wholesale Janitorial Supply. For sales, press one. For customer service, press two. To track your order, press three. To speak with our billing department, press four. To speak with the operator, press zero." The funny thing was, they all went to the same place—I was answering all of the lines! But the perception was that we were a large company with multiple departments. As a result, I had an unbelievable conversion rate and did an incredible amount of business. Nobody had to know that only two people worked there.

  There are many inexpensive, cloud-based, private branch extension (PBX) phone systems from which to choose. Do a Google search for "cloud phone system" to see which option best suits your needs.

- **Step Six: Have a LinkedIn Presence**

  Every business professional should have a LinkedIn profile. It should feature your headshot and provide your education, your employment history, and any other notable information about you. The summary is one of the most important parts of your profile, and also the most difficult to write. That's why I always hire a content writer to write my bio for $50. In fact, I pay content writers $50 each to write bios for every employee I hire.

- **Step Seven: Present Yourself as an Expert**

  Become an expert instantly by writing articles, posting them on other people's websites, and having your professionally written bio, your great headshot, and a link to your impeccable website.

  Again, consider hiring a content writer. For $50 to $250, a professional writer will craft a clear version of your brilliant insights and ideas.

  I have written and been mentioned in articles for numerous online industry publications and blogs, such as *Forbes, The Huffington Post,* and *Entrepreneur,* and there are multiple benefits. I highlight the articles I've written on our company press page to build social proof, and it is one of the best ways to build links to your website. Links from online publications are one of the most valuable ways to improve your website's ranking in search engines.

- **Step Eight: Invest in a Professional Address**

  So you found the perfect potential client—let's call him "Jim." You wrote the proposal, and Jim gave you a verbal "yes." This is the biggest deal you've ever had—a $30,000 contract! Before you pop that bottle of champagne, however, you send over the contract to Jim and wait for the signed document to be mailed back. A week goes by and you still haven't heard from Jim. You begin to get nervous. Then, a few days later, Jim calls to tell you, "I'm so sorry, but our legal team did some due diligence and they discovered that your address was a residential location. I like you, but our team is concerned about your capacity." No more champagne, no more $30,000 contract, all because you didn't have a professional address! A deflating experience, to be sure, and one that could have been avoided for only $99 a month through companies such as Regus.

This may never happen to you, but why roll the dice? Having a professional address offers you the following:

1. A professional address for you to receive mail.
2. A professional environment for you to meet with clients. Rather than having to meet at a coffee shop or home office, you can reserve a meeting room at your office location. Plus, if a client comes to see you and you're not there, a front desk assistant will tell the client you're out of the office, sparing you the embarrassment of someone coming to your house.
3. More financing options. There are a number of finance companies that will not provide you a loan or credit line if you don't have an office location.

While this will meet your needs initially and prevent you from experiencing the disasters mentioned above, it's not a permanent solution. As your company grows in revenue, I suggest getting a traditional office. Branding is about playing offense and defense. You have to first build your brand, and then you have to protect it! Having a professional office will help you with that.

The Takeaways

Say that you're the best at something. Say that you're the expert. Say that you are number one. Eventually, you will be.

The points discussed in this chapter help promote that perception of expertise and legitimacy in both your mind and your customers' minds. They are easy and inexpensive to implement, but many business owners neglect them. I put them in order for you, the reader, so there are no longer any excuses. This is the foundation you need in order to create a system that sells for you.

Questions for Consideration

1. What is your ultimate goal for your business?
2. What do you want people's perception of you and your business to be?
3. What is the vision for your company's brand?

CHAPTER 2

SOCIAL PROOF: BUILDING CONSUMER TRUST

What motivates people into making a buying decision? If you think everyone makes decisions based on pure logic and reasoning you would be sorely mistaken, especially if you were in sales. I learned this lesson when working at Metlife as a financial advisor after college. The head of the agency Marty Battock, took me under his wing and we would go on sales calls together. On one occasion, we met a husband and wife that had three kids in their home, and Marty as usual would let me present first. I spent half an hour presenting a complete financial plan with data proving what products would best protect their family. After I presented all the data and my recommended plan, they just shook their heads and said they needed to think about it. Then Marty took over. He told a story about another family that was his client years ago, about how he personally delivered the life insurance check to the family days after the father passed away from a heart attack; how that life insurance check allowed there to be food on the table for their three kids; and how all three kids have since graduated from college, all paid for by that life insurance policy. Marty then asked the husband in a kind and gentle voice, do you love your family? Both the husband and wife nodded and we started the paperwork. I remember in the car ride home I asked Marty why my pitch didn't work. Marty responded, "people buy from emotion."

In his book *Influence* (HarperCollins, 2009), Robert B. Cialdini discusses the theory of "social proof," a psychological phenomenon in which people mimic the actions and ideas of others in an attempt to exhibit the "correct" behavior. Advertisers have found they can influence the actions of people by creating the perception, whether true or false, that many people are doing the same thing.

People look for cues from those around them, so there is weight in reviews from consumers who have gone through the same research process. In any given social situation, about 50 percent of people actually make decisions and the other half follow their cues without even thinking about it.

When commercials tell you that four out of five dentists agree or when a book is marked with a "New York Times Best Seller" sticker, there is evidence that many others have already jumped on the bandwagon, making you more likely to do so too.

Have you ever wondered why your favorite sitcom uses an annoying laugh track? Because it works. Studio executives discovered that they could increase the perceived humor of a show just by playing canned laughter at key moments. In fact, shows that use a laugh track are perceived as funnier than shows that don't, even though viewers find it irritating. You laugh when the audience laughs, even when the audience isn't real. This is social proof in action.

As marketers, our goal is to establish enough social proof to encourage others to jump on that bandwagon, leading to more business.

While one demonstration of social proof certainly impacts behavior, when the same feedback comes from multiple sources, the effect is amplified. In a recent study, researchers observed that people who heard five positive book reviews read by five different voices rated that book more favorably than people who listened to the same five reviews read by just one voice.[1] The perception that those positive reviews were coming from a number of individuals made them more valuable to listeners. Think about when your newspaper's film critic, your best friend, and the Academy Awards nominating committee all endorse a movie; your tickets are as good as bought. We call this the **multiple-source effect.**

In addition, when people believe they share characteristics with those on board, the phenomenon of social proof is even more evident. This is called the **similarity effect.**

As you know, building a rapport with your customer or client is crucial, and you can do that effectively by playing up the connections between you and your target audience. When you visit a doctor and see his medical degrees on the wall and photos of his wife and kids on his desk, those images serve as social proof and potentially evoke the similarity effect. He has a degree from an Ivy League medical school, so he must be very intelligent. What's more, he has a wife and kids, which makes him instantly relatable if you also have a wife and kids. Trust has been established even before your conversation begins.

Leveraging social proof, both directly and indirectly, is one of the most important steps you can take to promote your business. If you can successfully demonstrate your value by using

---

1   Lee, Kwan Min (1 April 2004). "The Multiple Source Effect and Synthesized Speech." *Human Communication Research.* **30** (2): 182–207. doi:10.1111/j.1468-2958.2004.tb00730.x.

social proof and the factors that enhance it, you can charge a premium for your services, and you won't have to rely on price to compete in the marketplace. Plus, the return on your investment is often tenfold.

Let's say you're invited to do a television interview about your new restaurant. This is a terrific opportunity that you should take advantage of. The simple fact that you were invited to be on television is a very strong form of social proof, because it indicates that someone of influence found your restaurant worthwhile enough to put on television in the first place.

But maybe you're hesitant to participate. You're a little bit camera shy. You think to yourself, *How many people are really going to see this program that airs at 6:00 a.m.?* You're considering the direct influence, which may actually be minimal; perhaps there aren't very many people awake and watching at 6:00 a.m.

But the indirect influence of that interview is remarkable and long-lasting. If you put the clip on your website, that interview can work for you for years to come, and you've added yet another piece of social proof to what is hopefully a growing collection.

The problem is, people often don't take the extra step to collect and display their social proof, and they end up losing out on the potential to influence people long term. Many business-people are reluctant to offer social proof for a number of reasons. Some fear that showing evidence that others have endorsed their product or service will be interpreted as bragging. Others don't see its worth because the return on investment (ROI) is not directly measurable; it's hard to gauge emotional impact. But that emotional punch is also why social proof is so effective.

After decades of running businesses and marketing endeavors, I know that the psychological value and monetary return associated with social proof is significant. In this chapter, I'll provide you with some ways to leverage this invaluable phenomenon, with minimal investments that majorly maximize your return. I'll also provide the estimated value of each method. I've come to these numbers after many years of trial and error across multiple businesses. I offer them to you to give you an idea of what your time and energy could be worth, so that you can decide which tactics might be right for your business and your needs.

Seal In Trust

When I began running e-commerce websites, my first priority was to earn my customers' trust and protect their personal information. To do so, I had to purchase Secure Sockets Layer (SSL) certificates that would encrypt my websites, particularly pages that collected credit card information.

GoDaddy sold an SSL certificate for $70 per year, while Norton's was $700. The only difference I could see between the systems was that the more expensive one offered a more recognizable security seal that could be displayed on the website. It was hard for me to justify paying almost ten times more for what I perceived to be the exact same thing.

While simply stating that I was protecting customers' information via encryption served as social proof, I soon came to realize that the more expensive certificates had additional value in the form of those seemingly overpriced website seals. When I finally displayed the seal prominently on a checkout page, people felt more secure, and were therefore more likely to buy. With the more recognizable and expensive seal, I saw a 20 percent increase in completed orders, and the seal paid for itself. Studies have actually proven that displaying SSL seals delivers a significant

ROI.[2] Now, I always pay for premium SSL certificates because I know that I'll make that money back many times over.

In addition, the certificate you choose—and thus the one that appears on your checkout page—directly affects your conversion rate. While a lesser-known GoDaddy certificate might increase your conversion rate by one or two percent, numerous studies have shown that a Norton certificate can increase your rate by as much as 15 or 20 percent.[3] Norton has already established social proof and become a well-known presence on the Internet, and its easily recognizable seal imparts a level of competence and safety that is paramount to customers.

I often spend up to $1,000 on an SSL certificate from Norton and display it right at the top of a website. I've seen it increase my conversion rate by 20 percent or more. To me, that's worth at least ten times what I paid for that certificate.

Studies have also shown that when there is not a secure certificate on a website's checkout pages, companies lose 15 percent of sales or more.[4] And today, Google is even giving higher rankings to websites with secure pages. If you collect any kind of personal information—names, e-mail addresses, phone numbers, credit

---

2   John Stevens, "How Trust Factors Influence Online sales and Conversions," Internet Retailer, June 20, 2016, https://www.Internetretailer.com/commentary/2016/06/20/how-trust-factors-influence-online-sales-and-conversions.

3   Marie Dean, "Why Choosing the Right Trust Seal Increases eCommerce Conversions," CrazyEgg, August 22, 2014, https://blog.crazyegg.com/2014/08/22/trust-seal-ecommerce/.

4   "85% of Online Shoppers Avoid Unsecured Websites," GlobalSign Blog, November 19, 2014, https://www.globalsign.com/en/blog/85-of-online-shoppers-dont-buy-on-unsecured-websites1/.

cards, or other information—you definitely want to demonstrate that your site is secure.

Verification and malware seals also help to build social trust by assuring customers that your site is safe. Malware seals cost between $500 and $600 per year but are worth five to ten times the cost, especially if you are collecting personal information. I use Trust Guard Trust Seals on my websites. Trust Guard provides three different seals: One verifies your website has been scanned for viruses and malware. Another confirms that your business has been verified. And the third ensures customers that your website is secure.

You can also invest in a shopping guarantee, a seal that is activated after every purchase, and states that each purchase is guaranteed by a third party. I use Norton Shopping Guarantee for some of my websites, which assures customers that if they can't fix something with us directly, they have the added security of Norton's shopping guarantee. These seals cost between $500 and $1,000 a year, but if you have an e-commerce website, a shopping guarantee from a reputable company can be worth upward of $10,000 from increased conversion rates. A new option from Google is the Google Trusted Stores program. It works the same as the Norton Shopping Guarantee, though it's offered free from Google. It isn't easy to get—Google requires approximately 1,000 orders in three months to pass verification—but it's a powerful symbol.

While many seals come with the social proof that can turn trust into business, I recommend avoiding Payment Card Industry (PCI) compliance seals. Businesses that make more than a million dollars a year in revenue are sometimes required to purchase these. They're often very expensive, and as far as trust seals go, I don't think they're worth it. At a cost of up to $5,000 per year, you rarely recoup the loss.

Always make sure that your seal images work properly, so that when customers click on them, they're taken to a verification site; otherwise, it's just a hollow image.

When people buy life insurance policies from me, I ask them why they chose True Blue. The most common answer is, "You seemed trustworthy." I love hearing that, because it shows that the social proof we've built through seals and other guarantees is working.

Bank Your Testimonials and Reviews

Testimonials and reviews are a terrific and easily acquirable form of social proof. All businesses should feature a well-designed testimonials page on their websites. I include real customer feedback front and center whenever possible, resulting in conversion rates that are ten times better than my competitors. A link to your testimonials page should appear in the main menu, the main navigation bar, and the footer. Consider it an investment; testimonials last well beyond five years. An experienced designer or developer can format the page for around $250, or you can use software to manage your testimonials yourself for less than $100. Either way, it's worth it.

How do you collect testimonials? All you have to do is send an e-mail to your happy customers and ask them for a brief statement. If you've developed a relationship with your clients and they like your service, they'll be more than happy to share their experience.

To demonstrate validity, each testimonial must include a name, date, and location. Testimonials should be arranged by date, with the most recent one appearing first. Including an individual's location helps those reading the testimonial to feel a sense of similarity, knowing that these reviewers are people like them, living somewhere in the same country or perhaps even in the same city.

A star-rating system is a simple way to help people remember your reviews when they talk about your business with friends. Another indirect benefit of stars is that search engines can display them in their results; with the right code, the number of reviews and average rating will appear in Google search results.

You might be reading this and thinking that what I've just described requires a significant investment, when you include time. And what is the ROI? Well, every single testimonial that I collect and control has a value of $100 initially, and then an additional $50 per year. I came to this value based on the increase in conversion rates that each testimonial brings. So the more you get, the better. If you have ten testimonials on your website, you could be looking at a minimum of $500 to $1,000 in value each year. Aside from the indirect value of building trust and similarity, including a testimonials page on your website lets people know that you care about your customers' opinions. Your accountability is worth every penny.

Encourage Praise on Third-Party Sites

Third-party testimonials and reviews like those on Yelp, TripAdvisor, and Google are a little more difficult to acquire, but they're even more valuable than those you collect yourself. When people look up your business and find reviews on another site, your company has officially been vetted by an outside source. In addition, because of the ubiquity of the sites and the authenticity of their content, they rank very well on search engines. And, because you can't control them, they carry significant weight, meaning a third-party review can be ascribed a substantial monetary value. Each review that you get on sites like the Better Business Bureau, Google, Bing, or Yahoo, can be valued at around $250. I have found that one of the last steps a customer makes before purchasing is looking up your business on third-party review sites.

I have made it a point of obtaining Better Business Bureau and Google reviews for my life insurance business. If you look up "True Blue Life Insurance reviews" in Google, you will see my listings on these third-party sites show up first. More important, you will see a huge number of positive reviews of my company in these listings. We'll discuss the impact of user reviews in more detail in chapter three.

Include a Portfolio and List of Clients

Over the years, I've worked with many design and development companies. When I'm selecting a company, I always check to see who its clients are. If I can't easily find a list, I assume that either the company doesn't have many clients or it's not proud of the work it has done for them.

A page listing clients should be part of any company's website, and it should be easily accessible from both the site's main menu and its footer. Use high-quality, professional photographs, and consider hiring a designer to create an attractive template for the page at a cost of $150 to $500.

You should also include a portfolio of your work. If a portfolio doesn't fit your particular business, consider including case studies or "before and after" stories to serve as testaments to the quality of your products or services. Including references on these pages allows you to skip that step in the sales process, quickening each client's trip down the pipeline from prospect to customer. It also shows that you're proud of your work and that you have significant experience. A portfolio and clients page can easily be valued at over $10,000 when considering the increased sales they bring your business.

Invest in Partnerships and Endorsements

Can you imagine paying Kim Kardashian West $50,000 to come to your club for just one night? Probably not. But like the television interview we discussed earlier, your club would acquire significant indirect value simply because Kim Kardashian West went there one time. The photos from Kim's evening would probably appear in the media, and you could display them on the wall of your club and in marketing materials for many years to come.

While it may be difficult to get Kim into your business, you can tap into a similar type of cachet by partnering with prominent businesses. For the $50 it costs to pay a designer, you can add the names and logos of the major companies you're associated with to your website, even if they're just companies you buy from. For example, if you're a hairstylist who uses Paul Mitchell products, list the brand on your website. The company has already done all of the legwork of building its reputation, and listing the name of the company on your site allows you to leverage the social proof that company has built, in addition to your own. The increased sales from displaying reputable brands on your website can potentially be worth thousands of dollars.

Show User Statistics and Subscriber Accounts

User statistics and subscriber accounts are a popular way of showing that a company is popular or well established. A lot of companies include statistics that flatter their business. Almost every McDonald's posts a sign stating "Over 99 Billion Served." What

Brian Greenberg | 23

does this number reference? At first glance, you might think they have more than 99 billion customers—an impossible statistic, considering this is more than ten times the world's population. While the statistic is not necessarily clear and could potentially reference the number of individual French fries served, it's hard not to be impressed. A law firm might say that its lawyers have "150 years of combined experience." They could have five seasoned professionals in their firm, or they could have 150 lawyers, each with one year of experience. The point is, they're using statistics and numbers to build social proof that demonstrates they've done this before. Consider how the numbers you have might create the story you want to tell.

On my janitorial supplies website, I state that we've sold over $10 million in products. The main page of my insurance business's website informs customers that I've sold thousands of life insurance policies. Any time you have a chance to highlight compelling user statistics, you should.

How much is this worth? It's hard to say. It doesn't cost much to include these numbers, and it's usually at your own discretion—but it will cost less than $100 to put statistics on your website. Considering this information can result in thousands of dollars in increased sales, why not include your statistics?

Tout Your Press and Media Mentions
Press and media mentions promote you not only to your customers, but also to everyone with whom you do business. While most people wait for the press to come to them, I don't. It's possible that the local paper might get wind of an unbelievable story surrounding your business, contact you, and put you on the front page, but 99.9 percent of the time, you need to do the work yourself.

There are editors and writers for every media form, but they have to be pitched. I've learned that public relations is one of the best ways to build social proof, and that the indirect benefits from press and media make it totally worth the effort.

It's important to note that all of the forms of social proof we've discussed thus far make it easier to get press and media mentions. So, the more Twitter followers, e-mail subscribers, and reviews on third-party sites I have, the easier it is for me to become a guest contributor for a prominent publication.

Once I've established other forms of social proof and built up my reputation among peers, I come up with a pitch to help promote my business. Many people create lists: the top five reasons you should get life insurance, the top five ways to prevent getting the flu this season, the top five reasons to invest in SEO. These formats enable you to provide interesting information that is easily consumable. Once you draft your list, you can contact the editors at various media outlets and see if they'll pick up the story.

You can also hire a PR firm or publicist online. The cost of PR could be $10,000 or more a year, but it pays off: The value could be upward of $50,000. It's one of the better investments you can make in your business and has multiple benefits. PR firms have strong connections throughout the media world, enabling you to place an article in a major publication and bring in more business. You can further leverage that social proof by putting links to your media mentions on your website's press page. Additionally, links from media websites—especially if they're from high-authority sites—can increase search engine rankings significantly.

I value having a press mention on Forbes's website at upward of $5,000. The value is derived from the social proof I gain by displaying the mention on my press page and the increase in search engine rankings that Forbes's coveted link provides.

Other forms of media are also incredibly valuable. I've done a lot of radio interviews, and while I wondered how many people would tune in, I knew there would be indirect value in putting a link to that radio interview on my press page. If I do an interview for a local news radio station that is affiliated with CBS, I can put CBS's logo on my press page and include a copy of the show's audio.

Television appearances are even more valuable. Can you imagine your accountant being one of the experts on CNN or Fox Business? Wouldn't seeing her in that role increase your confidence in her abilities? It's always worth it to pay a few hundred dollars for the rights to display the clip, as the potential ROI and increased sales can be worth $10,000 or more.

The Takeaways

Your business's website is not the place to be humble. In the words of social-media expert Guy Kawasaki, "If you don't toot your own horn, don't complain that there's no music." While building social proof through trustworthy practices, happy customers, and positive press, make certain to display the proof on your website. Don't make your customers do the research on their own when you can do a far better—and more convincing—job.

On True Blue's website, I have a press page, a Better Business Bureau logo, an SSL certificate with extended validation, testimonials, my awards, a list of all the associations I belong to, and social-media statistics. I take advantage of every opportunity for social proof that I can, and as a result, my conversion rate is higher than that of my competitors. Because I have established myself as an authority, my bounce rate is extremely low, meaning those who come to my website do not look elsewhere.

Social proof builds momentum. The more you have, the easier it is to get more. Ultimately, your business will draw a crowd on its own, and the site will sell itself.

Work to compound your social proof through multiple channels; each form has its own value, and can continue to deliver a return long after you purchase a seal, collect positive reviews, or appear on your local news station. While there's certainly a cost in terms of time, energy, and dollars, I think you'll find that your results will be well worth the investment.

Questions for Consideration

1. How can you leverage social proof through your business?
2. What is your budget for providing social proof to your customers?
3. Think about the time, energy, and costs of social proof. What are some ways you can plan ahead and make sure you are making good investments with regards to social proof?
4. Which types of social proof do you feel best fit your business's brand?

Visit **brianjgreenberg.com** *to receive additional free tips, as well as more detailed information on recommended services and strategies.*

CHAPTER 3

THE IMPORTANCE OF REVIEWS

Customer reviews are a critical piece of the complex social proof puzzle, so this chapter aims to give you the knowledge you need to make it a powerful part of your business strategy.

Friends and neighbors have always asked one another for recommendations on the best dry cleaner, the best doctor, or the best Chinese food in town. But the big change in recent times is that the Internet has turned anyone with a WiFi connection and ten minutes to spare into a reviewer. We can now access opinions from people we don't know, who aren't necessarily professionals, just regular consumers like ourselves. Somewhat remarkably, we've grown to value those opinions.

Reviews, primarily those left online, are a determining factor for how an estimated 90 percent of consumers make daily purchases.[5] With the rise of social media and corporate transparency, we have a new, impartial source for learning more about

---

5   Stacey Rudolph, "The Impact of Online Reviews on Customers' Buying Decisions [Infographic]," Business 2 Community, July 25, 2015, http://www. business2community.com/infographics/impact-online-reviews-customers-buying-decisions-infographic-01280945#8tuyIu2LAuQc9C70.97.

products and services. And we, as business owners and service providers, can use that to our advantage.

In this chapter, I'll discuss how online reviews became so important and how you can master them to ensure that your product or service has the optimal number of reviews in all the right places.

Online Reviews: Furthering the Digital Conversation

Reviews have helped drive commerce for decades. Entire industries are built upon consumer reviews, from *Consumer Reports* magazine to the full-time food critic at your local newspaper. But now that anyone who uses our services can publicly rave or rant about his or her experience online, we have an opportunity to leverage these reviews as part of a marketing strategy.

The consumer review filled a gap that was missing from online shopping by adding another dimension: It provides a sensory experience from another human. When you're buying something online, whether it's an *Iron Man* T-shirt, Adele's new album, or a bar of artisanal soap, the purchasing platform only engages your sense of sight. Before you pull out your credit card, you probably want to know if that T-shirt material is soft or scratchy. How does the new album compare to her last one? What does the soap smell like? Now, thanks to user reviews, you have the ability to read what other customers have to say before you commit.

These reviewers are consumers, not shills. (Well, hopefully—and more on that later!) Usually, they've got no skin in the game, no reason to review other than to share their experience—good, bad, or indifferent—and perhaps feel the satisfaction of helping others find a product or service they like, or avoid spending money on something they don't. Their power and influence grows every time their insight proves correct. Some sites let you "rate" reviewers by telling them whether or not their review was helpful, or open up a comment box to thank or scold them.

Every time you buy a pair of shoes, see a movie, or eat at a restaurant based on a user review, you tend to trust reviews just a little more. In many ways, we're learning to trust anonymous online users even more than our friends. Don't believe me? Consider the following scenario: A friend tells you about his favorite Chinese restaurant. You nod, agree, and then surreptitiously whip out your phone and check the reviews. Everyone hates it. "Don't eat there," says one review. "We got food poisoning," says another. You find ten more rotten reviews.

So, whom do you trust? Do you listen to your friend, who you know likes his kung pao chicken on the spicy side, or the ten strangers who posted reviews online? Surprisingly, we take the reviews from anonymous people very seriously. According to research, 88 percent of people trust online reviews as much as a personal recommendation. We are particularly influenced by them if they provide details such as the date the review was written, their full name, whether they're a verified buyer, specifics about the meal, or pictures of the restaurant or dishes in question.[6]

Having one review is good—that certainly helps more than having zero reviews. But studies show that the more reviews you have, the higher your conversion rate will be for what you're selling. So, one or two reviews is good. Ten to twelve reviews is better. Fifty to sixty reviews is really gaining momentum. And

---

6   Rudolph, "Impact of Online Reviews..."

eighty to one hundred positive reviews will have a tremendous impact on your conversion rate.

The more proof and validity, the more we lean towards trusting these online reviews over the advice of our own friends. Whoever saw *this* coming? In this brave new world where strangers have outsized influence, we must adapt to the way users are really making consumer decisions. That means adapting to, and mastering, the art of the online user review.

Understanding the User Reviewer

So, who are these user reviewers? What makes them tick? Why do they spend their precious time leaving reviews online? Is it ego? Pride? A willingness to help others? These are the right questions to ask when you're trying to figure out the mentality of those who leave online reviews and those who read, use, and treat them like the gospel truth. Both mindsets are equally important to understand if you want to master getting, posting, and using online reviews to your advantage.

In his book, *Everyone's a Critic: Winning Customers in a Review-Driven World*, Bill Tancer explains that reviewers' personalities fall under four different archetypes:

- **The Communitarian** just wants to join the party. He is motivated by wanting to feel a part of a group or community, and uses reviews to participate. Often, a communitarian will add his two cents if he's had either a positive or negative experience; he believes it's his job to set the record straight for his people (who are, in this case, other shoppers).
- **The Benevolent Reviewer** just wants to help out, and hopes to boost businesses that provide great service with

her positive feedback. She may post reviews for family, friends, or places she frequents and enjoy.

- **The Status Seeker** is reviewing in order to build his own reputation, or to cash in on his opinion via free stuff, an elite title, or Internet notoriety.
- **The One-Star Assassin** is not interested in making friends. If she's had a bad experience, she believes it's her duty to seek vengeance or tell it like it is through a negative review.

Understanding reviewers' motivations—particularly their reviewing habits—is key to learning how to get better and more consistent reviews for your own product or service.

Digital Pride: The Reviewer Mentality

There's a growing sophistication among online reviewers. Sure, there are the odd few who leave one review and move on, but many get caught up in the cachet of being an "online reviewer." These are the status seekers Bill Tancer talks about.

Just as businesses build up a reputation by getting reviews for their services or products, consumers who make a habit of leaving reviews do the same. They actually enhance their profiles on several review sites. And these review sites, in return, reward reviewers for supplying what essentially amounts to free content.

In an effort to attract new reviewers, companies sometimes offer steep discounts to customers, or even free items, in exchange for reviews. In the Amazon Vine program, the reviewer is required to disclose that he or she received the product for free or at a discount in exchange for an honest product review. Not all of the reviews are in favor of the product, but from the consumer's perspective, this increases the validity of the reviews posted on the site. From the reviewers' standpoint, they see that if they stay with Amazon, they'll continue to get freebies.

Suddenly, you have folks who are considered "Super Reviewers" on Rotten Tomatoes, with their movie reviews appearing alongside paid, traditional movie reviewers from national publications like *Variety* and the *New York Times*. Someone might become a "Top 50" or "Top 100" reviewer on Amazon as a nod to their prolific habit of leaving reviews on verified purchases, a "Level 6" or "Level 2" contributor on TripAdvisor, or a member of Yelp's signature "Elite Squad." Status seekers can't get enough of these opportunities.

Savvy third-party sites—those not controlled by you, your business, or your brand, but independent of you—are seeing the power in rewarding reviewers for filling their site with user content. And reviewers are rewarded as well, not just with the special status of becoming a top, elite, or special reviewer, but also via discounts, free or reduced-price merchandise, free meals, and other incentives from businesses.

The Rise of User-Review Sites

Not surprisingly, review sites have been a boon, both to reviewers and companies seeking reviews. For reviewers, it lets them post, share, and "warehouse" their reviews along their entire network stream, from Facebook to Twitter, to their own blog. Some of them even become "professional reviewers," starting a movie-review blog, a book-review blog, or a jewelry-review blog.

Companies can broadcast a positive review, not just on their website but along their own social-media footprint as well. Every individual review becomes a new post, continually reminding followers, friends, and fans how people "just like them" think that company's product or service is amazing.

Savvier consumers can use review sites to dig deeper into a company's reputation. They understand that unscrupulous companies can use their own sites and affiliated sites to obfuscate the truth with testimonials that are edited, abbreviated, or even fabricated. These companies can trump up products to look like they've been reviewed by actual customers when they haven't.

Through sites like the Better Business Bureau, Facebook, Google, Yelp, TripAdvisor, and other third-party sites, consumers can scour the Internet to find a clearer picture. They can glean the "fake" testimonials on a company's website and find the real ones that exist elsewhere. In this way, review sites even the playing field for companies big and small, honorable and unscrupulous.

The dark side of customer feedback is that sites like Ripoff Report or Consumer Affairs can actually destroy a business. These sites exist to post consumer complaints. For instance, if someone posts a complaint on Ripoff Report, whether factual or untrue, companies can never remove it. Even if the consumer wants to say, "You know what? They fixed the problem. I'd like to take it off," it's impossible to get it off of that site.

Reviews Done Right

Amazon makes sure it's very easy for reviewers to submit a review for every purchase. Here are some things Amazon gets right about the review process:

- You can easily rate with the one- to five-star system.
- Customers' names appear in a review, shielding them from anonymity and eliminating the opportunity for trolls to simply leave one-star reviews for no good reason.

- Reviews show the specific version of the product that the customer bought. If a product comes in eight different colors, you'll know which color the reviewer bought.
- They sort reviews by dates.
- They organize reviews by which ones are "most helpful."
- They organize reviews by the number of stars and how many reviews there are for each number of stars. So one might say, "Well, there are a hundred five-star reviews and thirty four-star reviews, but only ten one-star reviews."

Some folks prefer to read all of the good reviews first. Some start with the bad reviews. They look for common themes or issues and make a decision based on the probability that they will be among the people who have had a good experience. Providing both positive and negative reviews enables customers to do the due diligence and research they need to make the decision to buy, particularly online.

On Yelp, just like on Amazon, you can click on users' profile names and see what other businesses they've reviewed. You might find that the customer submits terrible reviews across the board for everybody, which tends to invalidate his or her reliability. Or you may find that this customer reviews other places frequently, both good and bad, and is generally fair in his or her reviews.

Both sites provide a similar reviewing experience for different audiences. Amazon users are looking at products, while Yelp users are looking for establishments—hotels, restaurants, bars, etc. TripAdvisor provides these same services for the travel, hospitality and service industries. These sites take the reviewer community seriously, treating them with respect, which gives consumers a fair, unbiased opportunity to decide how to spend their money.

What's Wrong with Your Reviews?

For every site like Amazon and Yelp that gets reviews right, there's another that misses the mark. We've all seen the sales-y sites that make a big splash with testimonials that seem glowing, sincere, and "real" until you dig a little deeper. Often, these are small businesses that post testimonials with very little information about the "reviewer." For instance, they'll post a testimonial with a name and a position, but no date to indicate when the testimonial was given and no way to submit an additional testimonial.

You should also be wary of sites without star reviews, as star reviews have become an Internet standard. Research shows that 58 percent of consumers say that the star rating of a business is the most important part of a review, and that 73 percent of consumers think that reviews older than three months are no longer relevant.[7] A testimonial with no stars and no date does not look objective. Savvy consumers see that as a red flag. They will leave the company's website to visit a third-party site, where they will likely find not only many more reviews, but also less favorable and more factual ones.

That could all be avoided if the business's website simply listed honest reviews. If you're worried about bad reviews, go out and get better ones instead of fudging the best ones onto a fixed, noninteractive page.

Customer Service + Personal Touch = Great Reviews

For my businesses, I always list reviews very prominently. Oftentimes one of my insurance clients will ask an agent, "Are you the Jason that I'm reading all these positive reviews about?"

---

7   "Local Consumer Review Survey 2016," BrightLocal, August 2015, https://www.brightlocal.com/learn/local-consumer-review-survey/.

When the agent says "yes," the consumer knows that the person she has read about truly works for the company, and feels more confident about making an informed buying decision.

This can work in any business, not just the insurance business. Having an employee's name readily visible or easy to find—on a name tag, receipt, or business card, or in e-mail correspondence or a flyer—makes it easy for reviewers to include that name in their testimonial. Whether it's the name of a waiter, service representative, or agent, having a name in a review adds a personal element that just can't be beat.

The High Cost of Bad Reviews

Now more than ever, bad reviews can and will sink your business if you don't take action to rectify them. Consider the case of Amy's Baking Company in Arizona. They were on a TV show called *Kitchen Nightmares* with Gordon Ramsay, in which they were exposed for not baking their own goods, stealing tips from employees, and serving unsafe, unsanitary food. Management came across as awful people. Rather than fessing up and doing damage control, they took to social media and argued with people. The firestorm eventually forced them to close their doors. While this is an extreme case, the transparency and pervasiveness of social media can leave a business devastated by a few bad reviews.

I've seen businesses with negative reviews on the Better Business Bureau, Ripoff Report, or elsewhere that have built up such a bad reputation that they either went out of business or had to change their name and completely revamp their website to stay in business. Bad reviews can cost you tens of thousands of dollars or, worse, an entire career.

How to Handle Negative Reviews

No matter what business you are in, you will inevitably receive a negative review. While your first instinct may be to fight back and retaliate, **avoid retaliation at all costs.** There are few legal actions a business can take against a negative review because they are just opinions. Most attorneys won't even take such cases and if you decide to pursue legal action, it will most likely result in large losses of money and time.

It is also near impossible to get a review removed unless the reviewer removes it himself. Contacting Yelp, Google, or TripAdvisor to take down a review is simply a dead end.

The only way to win when fighting a negative review is to battle it with kindness, apologies, and pleas for mercy. I have seen so many business owners get into a dispute online with a reviewer, and the deeper and uglier the dispute gets, the more places that angry customer will post reviews.

When you get a bad review, you need to act immediately. Decide what steps you can take to convince an unhappy customer to take down his or her bad review. Can you replace the product for free? Offer a refund? If it's a service, can you fix it and get the customer to retract the review? Pursue all means necessary to avoid unknown damage to your reputation. While it may cost a little more to fix the problem, it will prevent additional negative reviews in the future, so isn't that worth it?

I believe companies should be willing to take up to a four-figure loss in order to rectify a negative review. Online reviews are much more important than the average company owner perceives them to be. According to the Local Consumer Review

Survey 2016 by BrightLocal, 74 percent of respondents say that positive reviews make them more likely to trust a local business.[8]

In my experience, responding in the appropriate way has turned negative reviews into positive ones. Negative reviews are an opportunity. According to a study in the *Journal of Consumer Research*, "politeness" in business responses can foster feelings of a more honest, down-to-earth, cheerful, and wholesome brand.[9]

Whenever a negative review arises, I suggest responding with five simple steps:

1. Apologize and sympathize.
2. Fix the problem.
3. Reiterate your brand's/company's beliefs.
4. Follow up and make sure the customer is satisfied with the result.
5. After the customer confirms he is satisfied, ask him to remove the negative review

A few years back, I found this all-caps rant on the Google business page of one of my companies:

DO NOT DO BUSINESS WITH THIS COMPANY! THE PRODUCT I ORDERED ARRIVED DAMAGED. CUSTOMER SERVICE WAS NO HELP AND ONLY OFFERED TO SEND THE

---

8   Local Consumer Review Survey 2016, BrightLocal...

9   Ryan Hamilton, Kathleen D. Vohs, Ann McGill, "We'll Be Honest, This Won't Be the Best Article You'll Ever Read: The Use of Dispreferred Markers in Word-of-Mouth Communication," *Journal of Consumer Research* 41, no. 1 (2014): 197-212. http://www.jstor.org/stable/10.1086/675926?seq=1#page_scan_tab_contents

ITEM AGAIN. IT IS TOO LATE AND I DO NOT
NEED THE PRODUCT ANYMORE! I WANT A
FULL REFUND FOR MY ORDER.
1 out of 5 stars

Although we had offered to rush-deliver a product to the customer at no extra charge, the shipping company we work with had damaged the product during delivery. When I spoke to the customer about the problem on the phone, I offered to ship him a new one. While he seemed pleased with that solution, he went on to write an angry review. So, I followed up with this message:

> I sincerely apologize that the product arrived damaged. It sounds like this caused major frustration, and we feel terrible about it. I have issued a full refund for the item you have ordered that will be credited to your credit card immediately. I have also added a credit of $50 to your account to purchase whatever you like.

> We do our best to pack our items as best we can and always try to exceed the expectations of our customers. Our goal is to make every customer happy, so please let me know if there is anything else we can do. I hope we get the chance to earn back your business in the future.

In the above response, I apologized to let the customer know that we are human and sometimes make mistakes. I rectified the situation right away by refunding the charge and by offering a credit to earn back his business. I then took the opportunity to convey that we are customer-centric and always do our best to make our customers happy.

The next step was to contact the customer and offer my apology and see what else I could do for him. My goal was to simply acknowledge his situation and do whatever it took to satisfy him. After that conversation, I asked the customer to take down the review. In this situation, he was able to do that.

If you can't get a review taken down, the best thing to do is respond to it. Most review sites allow the business owner to make a public comment in response to a negative review. This promotes integrity on both sides by not pressuring the customer to erase his comments, while providing the reviewed company a chance to tell its side of the story.

Make your most important points in the first couple of lines of your response, because usually that's all the site displays before readers have to click to view more. Let consumers know that you tried to fix the problem by offering some sort of solution or compensation to the dissatisfied party. In most cases, that's all people really want. We've all made mistakes or dealt with a customer who just couldn't be satisfied. When readers evaluate these reviews, they want to see that companies are doing what they can to acknowledge and solve customer issues.

Companies handle unhappy customers differently, depending on their values, and the policies built to reflect those values. Some companies believe the customer is always right, while others only want to get the money and could care less about the customer. If your company takes a negative review seriously, customers are more likely to trust you. Studies have found that people don't want to see all positive reviews. They want to see some cases where the business went out of its way to handle a problem. By doing this, you can turn a negative into a positive!

Elon Musk, the CEO of Tesla, Inc., ran into a big problem shortly after the company released the new Model S sedan. The company had to recall over four hundred vehicles at a time when Wall Street and Detroit automakers were looking for a way to squash the new car company.

Tesla representatives made house calls to every customer's home or office in cases where a recall was necessary. They personally picked up the car, left a loaner car, and drove the car back to California to fix the issue. They then personally delivered the repaired car back to the customer.

Tesla took this opportunity to show that owning a Tesla was not just about owning a great car, it was also about the concierge service that comes along with the car. While some thought the recalls would destroy the new company, it ended up creating great PR and brand evangelists.

How to Encourage Positive Reviews

Now that you know the importance of online reviews, it is up to you to be the "review cheerleader" at your company. Whether you're the CEO, CFO, VP, manager, or group or team leader, take it upon yourself to be a "rabid fan" of online reviews and spread the gospel far and wide. The promotion and maintenance of reviews needs to come from the top down and start from day one.

Make it an initiative to track and reward your team for positive reviews. Hold contests and offer a prize or bonus to the employee who receives the most reviews.

If you offer bonuses to employees, provide review benchmarks that they need to hit. Or simply offer a dollar-amount bonus for each third-party review received. When I wanted to make a push for Better Business Bureau reviews for my insurance company, I rewarded agents $50 for each review received. You will never receive what you don't ask for.

When you begin the sales process, let customers know that you value their reviews. The quicker you can get a customer to commit to writing a review, the better. Lots of websites have pop-ups that ask, "Would you be willing to submit a review after your purchase?" Customers can click it and reply, "Yes."

If you're talking to a satisfied customer, say, "I'm very happy I was able to help you. Reviews are a big part of our business. Would you be willing to submit a positive review on our website?" That ensures you a commitment, and the customer is much more likely to follow through with the review.

Many times customers just want to be heard. If you show them you're listening, they're happy. I know from experience that oftentimes customers want to make a connection with a company, not just "buy" from it. When I sell an insurance policy, I call my customers and let them know that I'm the owner of the company and I want to make sure they had a good experience. It may be a bit unorthodox, but I'll ask them for a verbal review on the call. Then, I'll dictate their words back to them and get their approval to post it. If there's a problem that led to a negative experience, I can fix the issue right then and there, turning a potentially negative review into a positive one.

Having a high-level employee call customers is a great way to get reviews, especially for new products or services that haven't yet been reviewed. Customers are often impressed to get a call from an owner and are happy to give a very positive review in return.

Be Accountable for Providing Great Service

One way to get great reviews is to make excellent customer service a priority. When great service is part of your corporate culture, there are fewer mistakes, fewer missteps and, as a result, fewer bad reviews.

A lot of companies say they want to be customer-centric. The best way to measure customer-centricity is by consumer satisfaction. Companies that allow feedback from customers are inevitably going to have better customer service.

Let's say, for example, that your employees talk to customers on the phone or via live chat. If you've implemented a policy requiring employees to ask consumers to rate their experience, there is inherent accountability. Employees know they're on the line for a potential positive or negative review from every customer, every time.

Great customer service and getting reviews has to be a priority for all employees. Moreover, employees need to be informed about both good and bad reviews, and recognize that there are repercussions for the bad ones.

Give Employees the Power to Fix Issues Right Away

I apply the golden rule of business to customer service. If I call a business with a complaint, the last thing I want is to be transferred to another department, or hear "I can't do that," or "I have to get authorization from somebody else." Empower your employees so that they are capable of providing a solution right then and there. Another issue that often arises with online sales is product returns. If you can develop a return policy that causes minimal stress for customers, you will build up a positive reputation in the online community. More often than not, customers won't leave negative reviews without actually trying to solve the problem. Negative reviews are usually due to poor service, not just poor products.

Where to Get Online Reviews

There are several ways to get, post, and curate online reviews. Here are some examples:

- **Control your own.** Curate the reviews on your own site. Make them real, get customer approval, and display them clearly, from the most recent date onward, so that consumers know they're valid and meaningful.

- **Post to third-party sites.** Sites like TripAdvisor, Yelp, the Better Business Bureau, Facebook, Google, and Superpages are third-party sites that curate user reviews. Encourage your satisfied customers to post reviews on these sites. If possible, reward them for doing so. If you target your happiest customers, you have the best chance of getting valuable reviews.

- **Feed your site.** Most third-party review sites have seals you can place on your site summarizing your company's aggregate review scores. If they don't provide a seal, I suggest creating your own custom seal that touts your reviews, and linking to your company's review page on their platform. Displaying various third-party reviews enhances those "controlled" testimonials already on your site. That way, you have a blend of controlled and uncontrolled reviews, giving your site greater legitimacy and balance. You're also giving your employees an incentive to make sure those uncontrolled reviews are as good as possible!

I always focus first on obtaining customer reviews that I can control. These reviews are from e-mail feedback forms that I send out. If a bad review comes in, then I have the opportunity to fix the problem and learn from the feedback. I also have the choice not to display the negative feedback on my site.

At my businesses, we only ask customers that have already given us five-star positive feedback through our internal review program to post on third-party sites that I do not control.

Use all three of these tools to constantly build up both product reviews and site reviews. Site reviews are those left by consumers about their buying experience with the company. Think of site reviews like a report card for your business. Product reviews, on the other hand, are just that: feedback on the product the consumer purchased. Although the nature of these reviews is different, the tools listed above can be applied to both. By doing this, you can provide transparency and information, while simultaneously building your reputation.

The Dollar Value of Third-Party Reviews

You might be surprised to learn that I value a great five-star review on a third-party site at $250. How did I arrive at that figure? Well, consider a few factors. The initial impact such a review makes is a positive impression, which encourages readers to look at other reviews and learn more about your company. The more time they spend researching your company, the less time they have to check out your competitors. One review gets the ball rolling and the momentum carries it across the finish line to make a sale.

Another thing to remember is that positive reviews on Yelp, Google, Better Business Bureau, or any other third-party site are around for a long time. They will inevitably increase your site's conversion rate, which adds to several additional orders and customers measured over the life of that review. When you calculate the lifetime value of several new customers, you can easily attribute a $250 value to a good third-party review.

It's like a free billboard that stays up as long as you're in business and creates a snowball effect. It's not just good for one sale, one week, one month, one year; it's more like one sale, every week, every month, every year.

And while a positive review—uncontrolled, random, and legitimate—on a third-party site is worth $250, a negative review is worth a loss of thousands of dollars. Yes, it's that costly. So you do *not* want a negative review on a third-party site to hurt your company's reputation. Negative reviews lower your conversion rate and lead to lost customers. People research a company's reputation on review sites as the last step before buying; one negative review is like a roach in a restaurant's dining room. As soon as the customer reads that negative review, he or she is off to your competitor's website and you've lost a sale.

I know the value of my reputation and my brand has gotten me online sales for fifteen years. I don't want to have to change my business name or answer questions about negative reviews. Do you?

Securing Reviews

Now that we're clear on the value of reviews, where do you get them? It's your job to let consumers know you want their reviews, make it easy for them to provide them, and then curate them. Here are some simple steps:

- **Send an e-mail.** I like to use contact-management systems like MailChimp or ActiveCampaign. These systems allow me to send e-mail messages to customers more than once. I can reach out seven days after a purchase, ten days after a purchase, and again fifteen days after a purchase, with minimal effort. Most e-commerce software comes with review software built in nowadays. So you can simply set up your e-mail preferences and let the system run automatically.

- **Offer an incentive.** Some people frown on offering incentives. From my experience, it's worth it because I know the value of customer feedback. The incentive could be a credit to their account or a discount on their next order. You can get creative when offering incentives to your customers. But remember, if you do offer incentives, **only offer them for reviews on a website you control** and that the incentives apply for honest feedback, both positive and negative.

- **Got tech?** Enlist technology as a tool to help secure reviews. For instance, I've seen people send an e-mail with clickable stars. When customers click on a star, they're transferred to the review site and can leave a comment. All they have to do is hit submit. Make it as easy as possible to take the first step toward leaving a review.

- **Call your customers.** This is an ideal tactic for companies just beginning to collect reviews. A method I've used is having an owner call customers to ask for a review. This is great for collecting positive reviews for the same reason that no one wants to tell parents they have an ugly baby. Conversely, if you want constructive criticism, it's best to have a lower-level employee call. Make sure you read back to the customer everything you wrote down, and get his or her approval to post the review.

Momentum is a powerful force in getting reviews. Once you start building up your reviews, you will generate sales without any additional effort and will be on your way to becoming a salesman who doesn't sell.

The Takeaways

Imagine a world where nearly all of your customers—a full 80 percent—make consumer decisions based on the word of their fellow consumers. It's not science fiction or fantasy; it's today's reality. You must quickly learn and utilize this resource to ensure that your own online user reviews will work for you. Here are some recommended review software and services, along with my personal ratings:

Shopper Approved: 5 stars
They have a very good system to garner reviews and use rich snippets, so that the star reviews show up in search results. They're also willing to customize the product or experience for new business.

Clients include: 1-800 Contacts, Quicken Loans, 1-800-Flowers, Web.com

Bazaarvoice: 5 stars
A very large player in customer-review software with high-quality service and high prices.

PowerReviews: 5 stars
Great review software that has been around for a while. They have been bought and sold a few times since 2012, but seem to be doing well.

Clients include: Skechers, Advance Auto Parts, Burt's Bees, CarMax, Autotrader, GEICO, L.L.Bean

Trustpilot: 4 stars
A new player to online reviews with a very good system. The only downside is that it's expensive.

Clients include: CitizenShipper, Check 'n Go, PetFlow, Express Watches

Review platform included with your chosen online store: 4 stars
Another strong option is to use the review/feedback system that is included with most major e-commerce platforms. The review capabilities included in sites like BigCommerce, Shopify, Magento, and many other online shopping carts have become very good over the years. They also have the benefit of being free.

Yotpo: 3 stars
This is a convenient plugin for many e-commerce platforms, and they're constantly improving their technology. However, Yotpo lacks the ability to gain both product and site reviews at the same time.

Third-Party Sites
Yelp: 5 stars
A great place to build reviews for businesses in the restaurant and service industry. The downside is that the long-term outlook is unknown; they could be irrelevant in three years.

Google Business Pages: 5 stars
The reviews show up prominently in Google searches and can bring in new business, especially for companies that operate in local areas because of Google's local search results. It's a great place to build reviews for the long term; Google isn't going away anytime soon.

Better Business Bureau: 5 stars
It costs about $550 per year to join the BBB. You can put their seal on your website, which builds trust. BBB listings rank extremely well in search engines, and their reviews display in the search results with visible star ratings. If somebody looks up your business by name, the BBB will be one of the top results.

TripAdvisor: 5 stars
Great for businesses in the hospitality industry. The site has millions of reviews and is a top destination for people booking travel plans.

Facebook: 3 stars
It is very easy for a Facebook user to leave a one-star rating for a business. The business must list its physical address to open up the review feature on Facebook. Additionally, those with poor reviews can easily turn off the review tab on their Facebook page. Not a good long-term bet for getting a return from reviews.

*Because of the volatile nature of the Internet, I recommend you visit my website, **brianjgreenberg.com**, to ensure you have the most accurate and up-to-date recommendations.*

Questions for Consideration

1. Which review sites or services seem viable for your business?
2. What incentives can you offer consumers for providing reviews?
3. If you are a small business or just starting out, how can you modify the necessary steps to protect your company from losing money due to bad reviews?
4. What is the best way to deal with customers' bad reviews of your business?

SECTION II

HOW TO GET FOUND

CHAPTER 4

SOCIAL MEDIA IS OVERRATED—FOR MOST BUSINESSES

You may have heard that, in this day and age, you need a social-media presence to stay competitive. While many businesses have invested in social media in recent years, it's important to note that social media might not produce the boost you're expecting. Conversion ratings from these investments are actually extremely low. In fact, despite its presence in our daily lives, only 1 percent of sales originate from social-media marketing. In this chapter, I'll explain for whom social media works best, how to make use of paid models, and how to employ organic, sustainable search techniques instead.

For the purposes of this book, I'll define social media as any website on which a user can create a profile and interact with others, and on which the business/group page owner can post news and updates to the community. Directory and review sites are excluded from this definition because they are not platforms specifically designed to have open discussions with users. We'll focus on industry behemoths like Facebook, Twitter, Instagram, Snapchat, and Pinterest, since these channels are often utilized by big and small businesses alike to varying degrees of success.

A few years ago, social media was believed to be the hot ticket, and companies often hired full-time employees to manage their accounts. They assumed that a strong social-media presence—the number of Twitter followers they had or the number of Facebook likes they got—would be treated much like links are treated, and would translate into higher search engine rankings. While intensive cultivation—typically one to five posts a day on each channel—and constant interaction with commenters might result in a high level of engagement, followers and likes do not directly affect search engine rankings. Moreover, for the majority of businesses, if these numbers have any impact on your ROI at all, it's often so miniscule that it's hardly worth the effort.

Social Media's Beneficiaries

For whom *does* social media work? It works for authors, motivational speakers, television personalities—people selling their insights, philosophies, and character. For instance, if you're a media personality like Robert Kiyosaki, Tony Robbins, or Kelly Ripa, increasing your interaction with fans across multiple channels can drive followers to purchase your books or invest in your platforms.

Knowing this to be true, when I became interested in writing a book about what I'd learned as a successful entrepreneur with multiple companies, I began building my brand on social media. I devoted time and energy to attracting new Twitter followers and Facebook friends who were interested in learning about my perspectives on business. Growing my social-media presence became a useful tool for establishing myself as a well-respected expert in various fields. Take as an example Fredrik Eklund from *Million Dollar Listing New York*. Eklund wrote a book called *The Sell*. By leveraging his enormous social following on Facebook and Instagram, his book hit the New York Times Best Seller list before its release date.

Other major beneficiaries of social media are upstart companies looking to raise brand awareness among their target market as quickly as possible. One such company is Probiotic America, which produces a number of nutritional supplements containing healthy bacteria. With an established national market, the company bought sponsored posts that popped up in Facebook feeds across the country. The content—a convincing, professionally produced thirty-minute video with beautiful graphics and research to back the company's products' benefits—not only raised Probiotic America's brand profile, but also netted many new clients.

Dollar Shave Club, a subscription razor delivery service, also raised brand awareness successfully via social media. The company launched a viral campaign featuring a highly entertaining and humorous video designed to convince people that they need cheaper blades for their razors, delivered directly to their door. In an even smarter move, the company purchased space for these videos on social media to raise brand awareness *before* spending big money on television ads. That way, it was able to test the model's profitability without investing too much off the bat.

Increasing Social Media's Potential: Paid Models and Sponsored Posts

It used to be possible to reach a desired audience on social media for free by building a large base of Twitter followers or Facebook friends who would then see anything and everything posted. But with new algorithms, only a limited selection of posts appears, so your followers won't even see the majority of your content.

Rather than investing the time and money in a full-time social-media manager to attract fans with a plethora of posts that no one will see, test the paid models. Buy targeted ads on Facebook and see if they improve business.

Have you ever taken a Facebook quiz that requires you to enter your information before sharing your results? If you've ever entered your e-mail address or clicked over to another website in order to find out which Disney princess you most resemble or which glasses will best fit your face shape, you've engaged with a sponsored Facebook ad.

Facebook ads have become especially effective tools. You can use them not only to drive traffic to your site, but also to collect contact information in order to add potential customers into your sales funnel. See if they work for you, but whatever you do, remember to start small.

Ask yourself who your customers are, what platforms they might be using, and how you can best take advantage of a particular social-media channel. Somebody who spends time on Facebook is looking to be entertained, which is why the Dollar Shave Club videos were so successful. People on Twitter are engaging with the present moment, which can make a well-timed tweet incredibly effective, and by the same token, quickly irrelevant. Instagram is more of a lifestyle medium, where immediately translatable, visual highlights play best.

Small businesses that find success on social media start with a very narrow focus. Spend your energy on one platform. When companies attempt to manage too many channels too soon, they end up diluting their resources and failing at all of them.

Once you know where your base is likely to congregate, you can try reaching them through pay-per-click ads. Start with just a few to measure your initial outcomes. Try investing 10 percent of your marketing budget in pay-per-click ads, or in paid posts on Twitter or Facebook. Remember, this is a temporary investment, and one you don't own. When purchasing sponsored posts on social media, keep in mind that the prices are always increasing, and the second you stop paying, they stop working.

While some paid models can work for some businesses, be wary of marketers who claim they can get your website to number one on Google by running your social media. Although I outsource certain aspects of my operations to save time and effort, I never do so when my brand and reputation are on the line. Letting an external marketer run your Facebook page can bring in followers who don't care about you or your company, amounting to numbers that might look good but serve little purpose.

If you do choose to run a social-media campaign, there are numerous ways to manage it without hiring someone full time or employing a marketing company. Software programs like Hootsuite and Sprout Social allow you to streamline and manage multiple social-media channels and schedule posts without constant monitoring. Since they require only a little time, energy, and money to operate, they can decrease your investment, while potentially drawing a return, and might be worth your while.

Go Organic: Invest in Search Engine Rankings

I'll explore search engine optimization in the next chapter, but for now it's relevant to say that if social media isn't all it's cracked up to be, a better route might be to consider going organic. Engage in the art of drawing in people who are interested in your business without paid ads. If you do the work and do it right, you'll bring in customers and clients who are ready to buy, with little or no cost. In addition, when you drive traffic to your business organically, your efforts belong to you. Every connection you create, every pathway that leads to your business is yours and will continue to work long after you've set it up, allowing you to sit back and watch the buyers roll in.

Here's how it works: Search engines have made it their business to get users to the most relevant results as quickly as possible. Your goal is to be the company that shows up first. Why? Because it's free exposure and advertising every time someone looks for a business in your category, whether you're a plumber, therapist, or wholesale coffee supplier. Most important, they're already looking for you, so the likelihood that they'll buy is high, sending your ROI through the roof. Even businesses that don't have websites can take advantage of organic opportunities for growth through third-party sites like Yelp, TripAdvisor, and the Amazon Merchant program. Investing time and a little bit of money in these efforts now will pay off exponentially in the long run.

Google deems a search successful when somebody types in a keyword, clicks on a website, and doesn't need to search again for another result. If a user clicks on the first link and heads right back to Google, it's considered a *bounce*. The average time a user spends on your site, combined with a low bounce rate, tells Google that your site is successful—a place where people can easily find what they want—and increases your site's weight in their search algorithm. While scammers and spammers might temporarily get to the number one spot using unscrupulous tactics, they won't stay there for long. Read more about SEO in chapter five.

Invest in What You Own

Rather than investing in social-media platforms that may or may not be around in three years, invest in your customer list, your search engine rankings, and your conversion rates. Instead of building followers, build your customer e-mail list. Your customer list is an asset you own, so collect e-mail addresses and use them to provide current and potential customers with quality content and information. A regular newsletter with links to your website can work wonders.

The Takeaways

You know your customers better than anyone else does. All of your communications and marketing efforts should serve your customers and reach them through the networks and channels where they spend the most time.

While social media can bring you attention, it's a short-term strategy on a platform that could be replaced by the next big thing tomorrow.

No matter what method you use to attract attention, the content you provide through social media, a third-party site, or a targeted newsletter should feel fresh and relevant, and it should keep you at the top of your customers' minds, so that when they're ready to buy, they think of you. With a strong system in place and multiple, useful pathways across multiple channels that lead to your business, you're on your way to sales without selling.

Questions for Consideration

1. Is social media really going to benefit your business? If so, which social media platforms are compatible with your business?
2. What are some of the other ways your company can be noticed that would work with your brand and budget?
3. How can you keep the content you provide through social media, a third-party site, or a targeted newsletter fresh and interesting for your consumers?

Visit **brianjgreenberg.com** *to receive additional free tips, as well as more detailed information on recommended services and strategies.*

CHAPTER 5

SEO MARKETING

Bob Berman, a family friend, owned a company that manufactured touch-free restroom and hygiene products—automatic flushers, faucets, soap dispensers, and air fresheners. At Bob's recommendation, my father became a distributor and began selling these products to local businesses. This was in 2001, and my father let me help part-time with the new business. Soon, my father and I were driving around Phoenix, selling to well-known restaurants and stores like P.F. Chang's, Fleming's, Walmart, and Costco.

We had two ideas about how we might improve our sales. The first was to provide the equipment at steep discounts and charge a monthly service fee to maintain all of the chemical refills. The second was to begin selling the products online.

I liked the idea of selling on the Internet—and it seemed like the perfect venue for my first attempt at building a business that would produce passive income.

We paid a developer $3,000 to build touchfreeconcepts.com (thank you, Shane Bailey!), and I went through the painstaking process of manually adding all of our products and content to the site. Unfortunately, I quickly learned that even the best website ever built is worthless if no one can find it.

I had to learn more about Internet marketing, so I took a sales job working for an Internet marketing company in Scottsdale, Arizona. Arizona was a hub for Internet marketing firms, and I was fortunate enough to work for one of the most successful of them all: Submitawebsite.com (now Web.com Search Agency). Joe Griffin and his son, Joe Jr., the owners at the time, introduced me to the new business of search engine optimization, or SEO. This was in 2002, and Google was just hitting its stride.

I was immediately drawn to the inner workings of search engines. I wanted to know how and why certain websites received top rankings on Google and Yahoo. I also knew that this experience could help me market our touch-free products online. I began investing in marketing for our TouchFree Concepts website, and in a few months we hit $12,000 in monthly revenue, all from organic SEO rankings on major search engines.

I remember telling my father that we had hit our peak in terms of revenue, because I thought the market wasn't going to get any bigger. I was very wrong. People started flocking to the Internet to do their shopping, and within a year we were doing $60,000 in revenue each month. From 2002 to 2010, it was like the Wild West for search engine marketing. Google had an algorithm to rank websites, but it still had vulnerabilities that could be exploited.

Google and PageRank: The Early Days of Search Engine Optimization

When Larry Page and Sergey Brin started Google, they created an algorithm to rank websites that used similar methodology to how medical journals were ranked: establishing which medical papers were the most authoritative based on how frequently other papers referenced them. Larry Page named this algorithm

"PageRank," by combining his last name with the name of the system used to evaluate the relevance of an individual web page. Google had hundreds, and later thousands, of ranking factors. But the most influential ranking factor back then, and still today, is the quality of the sites that "reference" or link to a particular website.

At that time, you could purchase a text link on a city newspaper site for $200 per month. The link would be placed in a box at the bottom of every page on the website. The box existed for no reason other than to trigger the Google algorithm to boost your website's rank. Google used to have a PageRank tool bar that would display the page rank of a website on a scale of one to ten. So, if the city newspaper site had a rank of seven, according to the Google toolbar, a link to your website from that page would raise your PageRank to six. An entire industry developed around link selling, and new marketplaces formed. Ads would read "PageRank 7 website link for $250 per month."

It was madness. Did I take part in it? You bet! It was how I found the best links and raised our website's search rankings. But all of that was short-lived. Google has come down hard on companies that buy links. Buying paid links these days can result in penalties that will send your website into the depths of permanent obscurity in the search engines.

SEO Consulting Services

By 2010, I had several businesses that were dominating the search engines in multiple niches. TouchFree Concepts was doing $1 million in annual revenue. Wholesale Janitorial Supply was doing $2 million in revenue. Another was making $600,000, and still another was bringing in $300,000 per year. I was quite the anomaly among my peers. I was able to take off any day of the week I wanted, and was not subject to the typical nine-to-five schedule.

I had already built my own network of websites that linked to each other in what I called three-way links. I wrote a program so that site owners could put codes on their websites that would link a group of websites, boosting their ranks. At the time, people were obsessed with link exchanges and reciprocal link exchanges, which meant contacting a site owner and asking if they'd like to exchange links. These were fine, but a reciprocal link was easily identified by Google and detrimental to your rank. I knew I had to be a step ahead.

The most powerful links are those from websites that don't link back to the original site. Armed with this information, I started linkbuildingsolutions.com. I had a sign-up page and instructions on how businesses could install the code on their sites. I divided the people who signed up into nonreciprocal groups. Group A would link to sites in Group B. Group B would link to sites in Group C. And Group C would link to sites in Group A. This format created one-way links that were difficult to identify and increased the search rankings for all participants.

From there, I started an Internet marketing company. It took me about eight months to have the website ranking at the top for some very competitive keywords, including the number one spot in Google for the search term "SEO services." This ranking alone had a value of about $100,000 per month in organic traffic. At its peak, the business had annual revenue of over $1,500,000. About 50 percent of this was pure profit. But I never truly enjoyed running the consulting business because of the large time commitment. I sold the company after just two years and began to focus on my other businesses that provided more passive income.

Panda and Penguin Google Updates

For years, business owners and marketing firms requested that links to their websites contain the keywords for which they wanted to rank. Since the inception of Google, marketers found the greatest increase in rankings using a keyword as text. You see these links all the time. When a site links to another site, there is some form of clickable text like "click here," the company's name: "ABC Corp," or a keyword such as "janitorial supplies." This text is usually underlined and in blue to indicate that it's a clickable link.

A famous example of the misuse of this ranking factor is when, in 2004, Internet marketers all over the world linked to George W. Bush's presidential biography page with the link text "miserable failure." For years, the first result in Google for the search term "miserable failure" was President Bush's web page. This was called a "Google bomb." Up until April 2012, Google maintained that it was not possible to penalize websites for incoming links. This was the general rule, because if links to your website could hurt rankings, your competitors had the power to send spam links to your site and lower your position. Google's written policy was that in the worst-case scenario, the links would be nullified and not count toward your overall site rank. But once Google launched its Panda and Penguin algorithms, everything changed. Google wiped the slate clean for many sites that had engaged in SEO marketing in the past.

While Panda penalized people for being part of blog networks, which were riddled with links from low-quality content, often generated by computer programs, the Penguin update penalized sites that had "unnatural" links with keywords. The Panda update was bad, but I truly loathed the Google Penguin update.

What had been the number one strongest ranking factor for years suddenly began backfiring for business owners, all thanks to the Penguin update. Thousands of sites were penalized for using previous SEO tactics, even if the links were genuine. I refer to it as the "Google Purge."

Let me use a hypothetical example to explain how this Google Purge worked. Picture a small business that specializes in selling gift baskets. An online news source writes an article on the best gift baskets to buy for the holidays, and features this small business. Capitalizing on the ranking factor, the company asks the news source to use the keyword "gift basket" in their article to link to their website. But if this gift basket company already has numerous other links with keywords (an SEO-wise company at this time could have hundreds of such links), this would trigger the Penguin penalty. It all depended on the overall link profile of your website. If you had just a few links with keywords in them, you could be all right. When you passed a certain unknown threshold beyond what Google deemed a natural mix of links, you were flagged for trying to manipulate their search algorithm and you found yourself in Google purgatory. Your site would drop in rank. Fewer customers would be able to find you in searches, and your business would plummet. While this example may be a bit simplistic, the point is that legitimate businesses were penalized for using marketing tactics that were once encouraged.

Once you triggered the penalty, there was almost no way to recover. Google did offer a way for site owners to "disavow" links that pointed to their websites in an effort to remove the penalty, but very few businesses ever recovered. I had a website that had a penalty and I ended up having to disavow 100 percent of the links to my site to remove the penalty. At that point I simply had to start a new website.

Most of my marketing clients fared well. I protected them from any Google updates, and built secondary websites for clients who were penalized. While these changes caused some initial setbacks, they provided me with a wealth of knowledge of SEO marketing that I can now pass along to you.

On-Page SEO vs. Off-Page SEO

Before we continue, I want to provide an overview of key concepts involved in SEO marketing. While it's not essential that you become an expert in SEO, it is important to have a general understanding of how and why SEO marketing works. In addition to the information provided here, I strongly recommend that you read the "Beginner's Guide to SEO" on Moz.com.

On-Page SEO

On-page SEO includes everything you can manipulate on your website to optimize rankings, such as:

- Design
- Content
- Search engine tags
- Internal linking
- Technical SEO tactics like alt tags, header tags, bolding, and keyword density
- Site architecture
- Additional information for search engine robots (301 and 302 redirects, custom "404 page not found" pages, site maps)
- Bounce rates
- Page load speed
- Mobile compatibility

There isn't room here to go into a lot of technical detail, but here are some basic tips you and your Web developers and designers can use to improve your on-page SEO:

1. Decide whether you're going to use "www" in your URL or not, and then 301 redirect to your chosen URL. If some pages on your site contain "www" and some do not, the search engine has to choose which ones to index. You want to make sure the search engine indexes the correct version. And, by having only one version, you'll reap the full benefit of SEO link building.
2. As a best practice, use mod_rewrite to end URLs with a slash and not the typical coding language abbreviation. This allows you to easily change platforms later (e.g., from "html" to "php" or "asp").
3. Include the page's keywords in the URL and use dashes between words.
4. Each page should focus on one to three keywords, which can include unlimited variations.
5. Use "relative" links in your site's code when linking to internal pages, like "/page2/" in case you move to "https" or change your subdomain.
6. The most important pages should be one click away from the home page; the more clicks away from the home page, the less ranking value the page gets.
7. Look at the title and description tags on each page. The title tag should be no more than 67 characters, and the meta description should be about 155. These can often be created dynamically using programming, especially on database-driven websites with hundreds or thousands of products.

8. Go over the main pages and make sure the main sections are identified as header tags—h1, h2, h3. These often need to be styled in a CSS file.

9. If you run a local business, put a list of the cities or states you serve in the content of your website.

10. Use "rich snippets" markup for the search engines. This allows the search engines to display everything from product review stars to your business hours directly in the search results. If you are a local business, you can use a rich snippets generator at https://www.webdesigners-directory.com/html/rich-snippet-structured-data-creator.cfm. Google has very useful developer guides that link to everything you will need here: https://developers.google.com/search/docs/guides/mark-up-content

11. Install Google Analytics code. I think it's the best analytics program available, and it's free.

12. Optimize the download speed for your website. Download speed is an increasingly important ranking factor. A good tool to find ways to improve your download speed can be found here: https://developers.google.com/speed/pagespeed/insights/

13. Finally, create great content. Content is king. The goal of the search engines is to rank the most useful results for each search.

Generating the Right Keywords

The most time-consuming aspect of creating an e-commerce website is writing quality content. You'll hear a great deal about selecting keywords—the search terms that produce results. It's amazing how much data is available regarding how often each keyword is searched.

I use SEMrush to discover the best keywords available. You can see the number of times a particular keyword is searched in Google each month, and also how much the keyword costs for pay-per-click ads. SEMrush also lets you see your competitors' top-ranking organic keywords and pay-per-click ads.

Some additional sites you can use to run some basic keyword searches are Google Keyword Planner (free, but clunky), WordStream (free, but with much of the data blocked out), and Ahrefs (which comes with a free trial). I also use AgencyAnalytics to keep track of rankings and Google Analytics.

Your home page should be the strongest page on your website, so use your main keywords for it. The keywords should be in your title tag and description tag, and within the content of the webpage. Make sure you have great content on your home page—don't think of it as just an entrance. I remember when websites often had fancy Flash videos with sound and moving graphics, which, unfortunately, made the most important page of their website completely invisible to search engines.

Choosing the Right SEO Platform

I strongly recommend you choose a popular SEO platform that is well supported for your website. WordPress is an excellent choice for sites that don't have e-commerce, specifically when combined with the Yoast SEO plugin.

WordPress is a great platform because there are so many plugins and extensions available, and the majority of plugins are free. I recommend purchasing a premium theme that has all of the technical SEO built in; these typically cost between $25 and $75.

When choosing WordPress for your website, make sure to keep your version up to date, and your content backed up. Hackers often target WordPress sites for vulnerabilities because it is one of the most utilized platforms on the Internet. If your site has e-commerce, choose a supportive platform like BigCommerce, Shopify, or Magento.

A Word of Warning about SEO Firms

If you choose to hire an SEO firm to help with your online business, the on-page SEO should be done by an experienced marketer. To improve ranking, it is sometimes necessary to modify the title and description tags, and possibly some of the content on the page to help with ranking, but changes should be made as part of a sporadic, once-a-year modification. On-page SEO work for a website is primarily a one-time project that should cost a onetime fee of $500 to $1,500. When you add new content to your website, do it yourself, or ask an SEO freelancer to create a good title and description tag for you. If an SEO firm tells you it must constantly monitor and change the SEO tags, the firm is most likely trying to take advantage of you.

If you have thousands of products, don't let anyone convince you that it's necessary to do SEO for each item on your website. E-commerce sites should be built using templates. When a website displays thousands of products, each product page is generated using your database. Global or site-wide changes need to be made only once to the master template, not to each individual page. Your site should comprise approximately four main template pages: Home Page, Category, Subcategory, and Product.

The title and description tags can be formulated dynamically from data in the database. You can give your programmer instructions like:

Title Tag:
[Product SKU] – [Product Price] – [Product Name] in stock.

Meta Description:
[Product Name] is available for immediate shipping to any location in the USA. Buy now for the best pricing available with a price-match guarantee.

The brackets contain data for each product found in your database. The text is static and remains the same for every product. I have seen companies charge thousands of dollars to formulate these SEO tags, which take about an hour to create.

Off-Page SEO

Once the on-page SEO is complete, it's time to focus on your off-page SEO, which is when the real work begins.

Off-page SEO encompasses anything you do outside your website to drive traffic and increase search engine rankings, such as:

- Pay-per-click campaigns
- Presence on external marketplaces (Google Shopping, Ebay, Amazon Merchant Services)
- Articles
- Blog posts
- Forum commenting
- Infographics
- Associations
- Public relations
- Contests
- Banner advertising

- Paid links
- Author bios
- Testimonials on other websites
- Social-media sites
- Review sites
- Videos
- Presentations

It's important to note that even though many SEO link-building tactics don't work anymore and can even invoke site penalization or a ban from Google, marketing agencies still attempt to sell you those old strategies, which will ultimately lead to the ruin of your website and require you to start a new one from scratch.

After the 2012 Panda and Penguin updates purged the Google index, Wil Reynolds from SEER Interactive introduced the term "RCS" ("Real Company Sh*t") during a presentation at MozCon, an SEO marketing conference. To increase page rankings, SEO companies need to do the same things that real companies do, rather than relying on tricks and cheats. Do real companies spin articles automatically with digital programs and pay to post them on blog carnivals and link networks? No. The same marketing strategies that work for major brands will work for your business as well.

This is a double-edged sword. It levels the playing field for those willing to put in the time and effort to gain natural links to a website, but it's not easy. You will often be required to promote yourself—even more so if you are in a competitive industry—and publicize your business far more than in the past. The good news is that it takes just a few high-quality links to set you apart from your competitors.

Links

Despite all of Google's algorithm updates over the last two decades, one thing has remained the same: Links still serve as one of the top determinants of organic rankings. Therefore, it's essential to maintain a concentrated focus on the links that lead back to your website. Any time a link to your site is listed by an external source, confirm that the link works by hovering your cursor over it. If you see the URL of your website in the bottom of the browser, you are good to go. If you see something unfamiliar, it's a redirect. A redirect links to a different page on the external site that *then* redirects to your website, which doesn't provide any SEO benefit to you.

The list of link-building strategies that will serve you in the long run and not get you penalized is short. Here are some of them:

- Business listings (Barnacle SEO)
- Site profiles
- Member and association profiles
- Testimonials
- Scholarships
- Charitable donations and sponsorships
- Guest blog posts
- Quotes and comments
- Link bait
- Evergreen posts
- Help from your friends
- Public relations
- Contributing authorships

We'll start at the top.

- **Business Listings (Barnacle SEO):** Make sure to begin your off-page SEO by placing your company in local business directories (Google Business Pages, Bing Business Pages, Yelp, Facebook, Superpages, The Business Journals, Manta, MerchantCircle, YellowBot, Whitepages, and the list goes on). These pages show up in search engines themselves and sometimes include links that head back to your website. Do a search in Google for "local business directories" to find current lists.

    When creating any business listing, always include a long description—at least five hundred words of unique content—especially for Google, Bing, and Yelp, as these directories display your business by location and relevance. How do they determine relevance? By what you put in the content of the listing! Far too many people create listings without inserting a lengthy, detailed description. I recommend a description that includes your main keywords.

    Some refer to this type of marketing as "Barnacle SEO." Wil Scott created this term in 2011 to describe the idea of attaching yourself to a larger entity and reaping the benefits of the resources it brings. Thousands of smaller businesses thrive just as a result of their listings on sites like Yelp, TripAdvisor, and Amazon.

    Take your listings seriously, treating them as extensions of your website. Include your photo or company logo. The more complete your listing, the better it will rank—and it only takes a couple of tweaks. I recently improved my accountant's listing with just a few changes. He had a Google Business Page listing without content. Once I added a good description with numerous keywords, put his business in appropriate categories, included some pictures of the owner and the location, and submitted a review, he began dominating Google local listings. So can you!

- **Site Profiles:** Never pass up the opportunity to create a profile that links back to your website on the industry forums or blogs you frequent. The descriptions are not as important here; instead, the links themselves provide the value. The individual profiles you create often allow for website links, as well as links to your social-media pages (Facebook, Twitter, LinkedIn, Google). I have profiles on sites like Moz, SEOBook, and the Insurance Library (http://www.insurancelibrary.com/). These links are also free. To determine if the profile provides a valuable link, do the following:

  - Make sure the profile pages are indexed by Google. Go to another person's profile and copy the URL. Then, do a Google search of the URL with "info:" in front of it and see if the page comes up. Example: info:https://www.truebluelifeinsurance.com/
  If Google has a cache of the page, the profiles are indexed.
  - Find a profile that links to the company's website and hover your cursor over the link to confirm that the company's URL shows in the bottom of the browser. If it directs you elsewhere, there is no value.

Note that social-media business pages are great, but are not particularly helpful for link building or increasing your site's search engine rankings.

- **Member and Association Profiles:** Member and association profiles provide another opportunity to link to your site, along with other benefits. When I join associations, I make sure to note whether they provide a link back to my websites. I particularly love associations that offer a seal that I can place on my site.

  Though industry associations sometimes have membership fees, the links and social proof built through their site seals are certainly worth the investment.

  I belong to the following associations, among others:

  - The Better Business Bureau ($550 per year)
  - Ethics.net ($156 per year)
  - Scottsdale Chamber of Commerce ($445 per year)
  - NAIFA (National Association of Insurance and Financial Advisors) ($500 per year)
  - The Million Dollar Round Table (top 1 percent of financial professionals worldwide)($550 per year)

  To find relevant associations in your area and industry, begin with a Google search. Search "[your industry] associations [your city or state]" in Google. Make sure the association provides a member-listing page that is cached or indexed by major search engines, as well as links. You may also decide it's worth it to sponsor the association if the cost is reasonable and the association provides a valuable link; this is what the big brands do. It's expensive, but a worthwhile investment if you want to be a major player.

- **Testimonials:** I often offer to write testimonials for services I use, especially when they provide a link to my business in addition to my feedback. If the service does provide links with testimonials on its site, take advantage of this wonderful opportunity to earn a strong connection from a high-ranking website. I always submit my review with my picture or logo, name, position, and website address. Make sure to provide all of the same information as the other testimonials listed on the service's page.

Include a simple introduction when submitting your testimonial through e-mail or by contact submission form, such as: "Below is a testimonial for your webpage at http://www.testimonialpage.com." Then, put the testimonial in quotation marks. If they don't have a place to upload a corresponding image, share it via Dropbox, or provide the image URL from your website. If they don't respond, resend. "The squeaky wheel gets the grease" is an idiom for a reason. Ninety-five percent of the time, someone gets back to me right away, thanking me for the testimonial and promising to put it on the webpage right away.

I've gotten testimonial links from my hosting company, SSL-certificate company, live-chat company, phone-service company, answering-service company, e-commerce–software company, and many other service providers for my businesses.

I often weigh whether or not I can get a link from a testimonials page when deciding which vendor to do business with.

- **Scholarships:** Offering scholarships is a wonderful practice for many reasons; among them is acquiring high-quality links from .edu sites. Establishing a scholarship doesn't take much of an investment; even $500 will do. Once you decide on the guidelines for your scholarship, make a list of higher-education websites to submit to. Narrow your list to institutions that meet the following requirements:

- Has an external scholarship page
- Is indexed by Google
- Provides links back to the contest holders' websites

To begin publicizing your scholarship, do a Google search for "External Scholarships," and send out a polite e-mail asking each institution you find to post your scholarship on their website. Here is a sample e-mail I send out:

Dear [Name]:

I would like to include our True Blue Life Insurance Scholarship on your scholarship page located at [scholarship page URL] under Video Contests. Our submissions page is located at https://www. truebluelifeinsurance.com/scholarship/.

This is a $2,500 scholarship with a submission deadline of [date].
Please confirm receipt of this e-mail so that we may provide your students with access to this opportunity.

Sincerely,
Brian Greenberg
CEO/Founder
True Blue Life Insurance

There are also several scholarship websites that list available opportunities by aggregating data from higher-education websites, but they do not provide links.

I personally like video contests because I can allow users to vote on the winner. Many people offer essay competitions and they become inundated with several hundred essays to read.

- **Charitable Donations/Sponsorships:** Another way to build amazing links—with the added benefit of supporting a great cause—is to become a sponsor of a charity or event. Sponsorships come with many perks, including marketing and branding opportunities in newsletters, on signage, and more. But these benefits are not really what I'm after. Whenever I sponsor a charity or event, all I ask is that a link to my website be included on the organization's sponsors page. Because I'm not in it for the signage or newsletter publicity, I'll often ask for additional link-related perks, like having my company link appear on the organization's website for a longer period of time, or including links to my other businesses as well.

  To request links from charitable organizations or events, you will probably have to donate at least $500, depending on the size and reputation of the organization. It's not cheap, but the connection is very valuable. Remember, you'll not only be supporting a great cause, but also enhancing your company's social proof by displaying your charitable activities on your own website.

  To find sponsorship opportunities, simply search for "sponsors" in Google. This is a great place to begin, as Google will filter for your surrounding area. Also, you'll know the pages are already indexed. If the pages listed provide links, you're in business.

- **Guest Blog Posts:** Guest blog posts can be valuable, although since they have been abused by SEO companies in the past, they've been targeted by Google under the Panda update. When doing a guest post, quality is far more important than quantity. Posts should be placed on strong websites that are relevant to your market. Do not, under any circumstances, guest blog on a site that accepts paid posts. It's extremely risky and will make your business vulnerable to penalties.

  When considering which sites to approach for a guest-blogging opportunity, look for blogs in your industry. Try searching your industry name, plus the keywords "submit a comment."

  You can also search the backlink profiles of your most successful competitors to determine where they've blogged in the past. Using information about what they have already published, come up with a few topic ideas. Then, contact the person in charge of the blog. You can usually find this by looking for the author of most of the site's articles. Send him an e-mail asking if any of the topics you have listed would be of interest. Let the person know this will be exclusive content, just for his blog. You can also draft the article beforehand and send it for his consideration. If the content is useful and well written, there's a very good chance he will post it on his site.

  It is important to clarify here that your post cannot be overtly self-promotional. There should be no links to your website in the content at all; instead, the link we are after is the one in the author bio at the bottom of the post.

- **Quotes and Comments:** By quotes and comments, I mean content you provide to external sites, most often on blog posts and articles, that can be used to link back to your page. There are several ways to get these links.

    One of the most accessible, but also one of the hardest, is to use a reputable sourcing service like Help a Reporter Out (HARO), www.helpareporter.com. Sourcing services like HARO connect reporters with industry experts. Sign up for this list and you'll get a good taste of how you can provide your valuable insight to interested journalists. The drawback of using HARO is that even if you submit a brilliant response, there is no guarantee that your input will be used—or worse, it could be used without a link to your website. Nevertheless, joining this site is a great idea, even if it's just to get a sense of the topics that are trending.

    Another strategy is to reach out to the editors of popular industry blogs. You can get this information by doing a Google search for your industry name, followed by the word "news." The same checklist should apply here as before when choosing a blog:

- Are the article pages indexed?
- Do they provide links?
- Can you find examples of them linking to other websites?
- Are the links clean of any redirects?

Once you've chosen an appropriate publication, send the editor an e-mail introducing yourself. Remember, this is not the time to be modest. Include as much social proof as you can. Direct them to your press page, portfolio, and associations. This is where all the social proof we have been building earns your investment back. Offer to create content and/or provide comments, expert opinions, or anything else they may require.

- **Link Bait:** Link bait is content that is so useful and informative, it naturally earns links from industry sources. The content might serve as a source for other posts, or it might be reposted as a valuable nugget for a site's readership. The rule of thumb is to shoot for "10X content,"—material that is ten times better than any other available information on the subject. The best link-bait guide I have ever come across is Moz's "10 Extraordinary Examples of Effective Link Bait," which I summarize below.

  1. Get influencers involved. Find the lead voices in your industry and ask them to provide a quote for the article. Often these influencers will not only link to your content, they will also share it with their followers.
  2. Make it easy to understand.
  3. Give away free stuff—primarily information. Links, tools, even discount codes are excellent items to offer.
  4. Create lists. What's more digestible than a clear, concise list that gets right to the point?
  5. Choose a highly desired topic. Find out what's trending on social media or on the news, and make sure your content capitalizes on the most current concerns.
  6. Generate personalized content. The more usable the tools you provide, the more people will interact with your site and its contents.
  7. Establish it as the go-to resource. Your content should capture the best information out there.

8. Make it visually appealing. Use clear headers, bold statements, and simple breakdowns to make everything easy to read and even easier to consume.
9. Segment large lists to make them readable.
10. Use social share buttons. Make sure readers have ample opportunities to share on social media.

- **Evergreen Content:** Another strategy for link bait is the creation of evergreen content. Like the tree from which it derives its name, evergreen content is continually relevant, never goes out of date, and remains fresh for readers.

In an article for Business.com, Larry Alston lists the five types of evergreen content:

1. Beginner's guides
2. How-to resources
3. Infographics
4. Annual or "best of" posts
5. Interviews

When writing evergreen content, keep your audience in mind. This material will probably be most relevant for industry beginners. Avoid using overly technical language and break down complex or broad topics into shorter, more specific chunks.

- **Help from Your Friends:** According to Keith Ferrazzi's advice in his book, *Never Eat Alone*, the best way to get help from someone is to offer her help first. Write an e-mail introducing yourself, offer to include a link to her website for SEO purposes, and only after you've offered your assistance, ask that she link to you. Here's an example of an effective request that True Blue Life Insurance might receive:

Dear [Name];

I work for the content marketing company ██████ ██████ and I'm writing on behalf of ██████████, one of the nation's largest insurance agencies. They offer consumers a comparison-shopping service to help them find great rates on auto insurance, home insurance, small-business insurance, motorcycle insurance, and more. We're starting a new Expert Interview series with important people in the insurance industry, and we'd love to do an interview with you and run it on the ██████ ██████ blog!

We'll send you a few interview questions, and we'll turn your responses into a great article for our audience with a link back to True Blue Life Insurance. All we ask for in return is a post on your site that promotes the interview and a link to our content.

You can see our website here: ██████████. If you'd like to discuss the program with someone at the company directly, feel free to contact ██████ at ██████@ ██████.

Please let me know if you'd be interested in doing the interview with us, and we'll get moving on it right away!

Best regards,
Susan

Reach out to others in your industry, even competitors. Introduce yourself and start building a network of friends. The most successful people in an industry often know all of the other people in it. All you're looking for is to contribute a simple quote to an article or blog post on their site, and a corresponding link going to your site.

Always offer something in exchange for including a link to your site. If you have a second site, offer to place a link there. This way, you can both help each other by generating valuable one-way links.

- **PR Campaigns/Campaign Marketing:** Public-relations campaigns are about creating great content that connects directly to your website. You want the content to be so interesting that other media outlets, blogs, and publications will include it on their websites. Creating content worthy of earning links is not easy. Moz did a very thorough research project on the subject, tracking over 300 content-marketing campaigns. These campaigns were built for the purpose of building links. Moz found that the most linkable content is highly emotional, has broad appeal, contains comparisons, and is pop-culture themed.

  Public relations firms will continue to play a large part in building the kinds of links necessary to increase organic search engine rankings. But many PR firms are not savvy about how to use their campaign efforts for link building. It's important to be clear that while you want PR for your press page, to attract new customers and build your reputation as an expert, you are also interested in the external links these campaigns can draw.

Traditional PR firms are extremely expensive, with rates that start at about $10,000 per month. Post a project on a site like Freelancer or Upwork, and you'll receive offers from qualified PR specialists that will provide services in the far more reasonable range of $500 to $5,000. I recommend finding a PR specialist who works in a smaller group.

As with guest blog posts, the focus of your PR campaign should be on link building. The content should not be self-promotional, and doesn't need to be. As long as your link is in the author's profile, you're golden. I've had success promoting content across numerous quality sources including blogs, publications, radio shows, and TV interviews. Your PR specialist can help you come up with ideas.

To begin dipping your toes in the public-relations pool on your own, I recommend contacting local papers or alumni publications for featured articles on your business. Once you locate some potential opportunities, I recommend reaching out via e-mail, and then following up with a phone call. Include a summary of your business, your expertise, and any unique position or new perspective you bring to your industry, and add an exciting hook that promotes your cause. Is your company offering a new spin on an old service? Are you customer focused, and how is that working out for you? Are you offering more transparency? Reach out to every relevant contact you can find. Many places are hungry for great content; you just have to let them know you have it.

I've had success in creating articles like "The Seven Life Insurance Game Changers to Look Out for in [Year]" and "Seven Pitfalls to Avoid when Running a Family Business." In my experience, I've found that editors love lists.

- **Contributing Authorships:** After you build up your reputation and social proof, you can become a contributing expert or guest editor for popular publications. This is where the indirect benefit of social media—having a Twitter or Facebook following—comes into play. If you have a large following, they'll be interested in the traffic you can provide. Most major publications have contributor guidelines and an application process. Provide your most successful press releases, sample articles you've written, and a summary of your accolades. Target publications that provide a link in the author bio. You don't have to start with the *Wall Street Journal*. Find industry publications first, and keep building until you've become the expert in your field. If you aren't a talented writer, find a freelance writer to help you create useful content. These are some of the most valuable links your business will ever receive.

The Takeaways

For SEO to be truly effective in the long term, you have to do the work. Using shortcuts and scams to improve your rankings is a thing of the past and can result in major losses. Building high-quality links through multiple sources is essential to the success of your website and, if done properly, can pay off big time.

While the list of beneficial link-building strategies is much more limited than it was just a few years ago, these methods are tried and true. High-quality connections earned from doing "Real Company Sh*t" will boost business and build you a network that will continue to deliver long after you've gone to sleep—even after you've retired.

Questions for Consideration

1. What are some keywords that would be valuable for SEO for your business's website?
2. What should you look out for when hiring an SEO firm?
3. What types of link-building seems like a good fit for your company?
4. Why can shortcuts be harmful in terms of SEO?

SECTION III

PRACTICE WHAT YOU PREACH

CHAPTER 6

TRANSPARENCY: A CLEAR ESSENTIAL

In 2015, I held a scholarship contest for high school and college students on True Blue's website. I asked applicants to submit a video about how to build trust and loyalty among the millennial generation and offered a potential scholarship award of $2,500. I posted the contest on the external scholarship page of every university I could find. You might wonder why I created a scholarship or why I'm telling you about it in the first place. After all, there's not necessarily a clear connection between life insurance and making college more affordable. But the contest benefited me in multiple ways (and a similar strategy could serve you too):

One: When accredited universities, which carry significant clout in the SEO world, linked directly to my website, my search engine rankings immediately improved.

Two: I used a software program that allowed my website users to vote on the best entry, saving me time *while* increasing engagement. With a little encouragement across my social-media channels, I drove people to the website to vote and made the process as hands-off for me as possible. It worked tremendously. People who had never visited my website before came to submit and vote, and those competing brought additional traffic by encouraging their friends to log on and vote as well.

Three: I got an influx of great answers on how to build trust among the millennial generation from millennials themselves! How do millennials believe trust is built? As soon as their submissions began pouring in, the answer was obvious: through transparency. In fact, "Transparency" was the title of the winning video.

Why is transparency so important? Why did it appear in video after video? Because as the Internet has become a more prevalent force in our lives—especially among the younger generation—people are skeptical of the validity of what they see online. The Internet makes it easy to do business anonymously, decreasing accountability and making it easier for companies to use loopholes and caveats to take advantage of customers. Millennials want to see reviews; they want to see visible business practices; they want to see proof that you run an honest business. The younger generation wants complete transparency.

The Inception of Internet Skepticism

It turns out that baby boomers also exhibit a fair amount of Internet skepticism. Having witnessed the Internet's humble beginnings, baby boomers experienced much of the early confusion and trickery associated with it. Consider the case of America Online (AOL), one of the first and most popular Internet services. In the beginning, AOL sold hours of Internet time, accessible through a household phone line.

As technology advanced, people began to use a cable connection for increased speed rather than their phone line. But when they tried to cancel their phone line service with AOL, they found it impossible.

There was no clear path to terminate your plan. If you called AOL's service number, you were put on hold forever, and when your call was finally picked up, nobody could answer your questions. The runaround was constant and the hoops were impossible to jump through, so much so that many found it easier to cancel their credit cards or close their bank accounts. This practice tainted everyone's experience and made a permanent imprint on the minds of an entire generation. To boomers, AOL was A-O-Hell, and for many, that perception extended to the Internet at large.

The anonymity made possible by the Internet continues to be an issue, and as technology advances, so do scammers. Someone may pose as a Nigerian prince or an elderly relative in order to earn your trust and steal your money. You might think you're talking to a beautiful girl online, only to find out months later that you've been catfished.

There are all sorts of dangers, including so-called Trojans (malware disguised as legitimate software), ransomware (software designed to take over your computer until a sum of money is paid), keystroke trackers, and credit card and identity thieves who can make your life miserable.

As more cybercrimes occur, skepticism will continue to rise. These days, criminals are more likely to hide behind computer screens than to rob you with a gun. **With today's Internet culture, the only antidote to customer skepticism is transparency.**

Though I worked hard to establish legitimacy and customer security in all of my businesses through reviews and other evidence, I quickly realized that many other companies falsify theirs. They post fake testimonials or buy reviews; in fact, Amazon is in the process of shutting down vendors that sell glowing—and entirely false—praise. People put fake seals on their websites—icons that are just images, rather than clickable links that verify authenticity. Some companies even post stock photos of nonexistent "staff" in an attempt to convince customers of their legitimacy.

Identity thieves send e-mail messages that appear to be from PayPal or your bank, requesting information to verify your account. The goal is to have you head to their website, which looks very much like the website of your bank, and voluntarily divulge your personal information.

Consumers are wary, and rightfully so. It's your responsibility to earn their trust.

Demonstrate Your Ethics with Evidence

As scammers evolve, your business's level of transparency must increase as well. Consumers need to know that there is recourse if the transaction doesn't go well. They want to know that the company has a good reputation, and one that must be maintained. They want proof of ethics, a customer-centric mission and philosophy, and a clear business model. Providing this much-needed evidence can set you apart—and close a sale.

Even if your hesitation surrounding transparency stems from the fact that you yourself fear spammers and hackers, there are a number of non-negotiables you must provide to your customers:

- **Provide your location and contact information.** Returning to a topic I touched on in the very first chapter, the number one piece of information that you need to provide, as a business owner, is your location. Displaying some sort of address provides an image of accountability. If you work from home, display your home address. If you don't feel comfortable displaying your home address, there are several virtual-office services, such as Regus, that can provide an inexpensive address for your business. I like to link to Google Maps so that customers can actually see that I have a physical address, and that Google can find it. If no address is given, the consumer will wonder what (or where) you are hiding.

The second piece of vital information to include on your site is your contact information. There are so many websites that don't show a phone number or even an e-mail address. Instead, they just include a contact form.

If customers can't connect with you on their own terms, there is no accountability, and probably no sale. The more contact information you can give, the better.

- **Offer third-party verification.** Prominently displaying third-party verification—seals, awards, and even trade associations that you belong to—increases your transparency and credibility; it provides proof that your company's reputation exists in places other than your own website. Link to your profile page on third-party websites. A broader presence on the web tells potential customers that you exist, you've been vetted, and that you're in it for the long haul.

  For my websites I display seals for our Better Business Bureau listing, LinkedIn profile, Facebook page, SSL certificate, business verification confirmation, malware scan results, Google business page, local chamber of commerce, and several industry associations we belong to. Do not be modest in displaying accurate third-party social proof. These are all integral pieces in displaying the transparency necessary to sway a prospective customer into doing business with your company.

- **Tell them your terms and conditions.** Another must-have is a clear list of "terms and conditions" that includes all of the ins and outs of your business. What questions are most frequently asked, and what are the answers? What are your return policies? By providing this information, you furnish customers with the answers they seek up front, so there's no need for them to ask. Further, this information protects both you and your customer should an issue arise. Once your guarantees are in writing, they are enforceable not only by your staff, but by credit card companies as well.

- **Protect customer privacy.** Many companies profit by selling customer information to other businesses. In the life insurance industry, these companies are called lead generators. After collecting a person's name, e-mail address, phone number, and sometimes even an address in order to run an insurance quote, they sell the information, or lead, to as many as eight different life insurance agents at a rate of $8 to $25 per name. The result? Those endless calls and e-mails whose origin customers can't quite pinpoint. Share your privacy policy, and assure your customers that you will not sell their information to other vendors or third parties. We create our privacy policies using FreePrivacyPolicy.com. It takes just ten minutes to create a professional policies page that contains all of the necessary terms and conditions.

Clear Content: Building a Transparent Website

Customers should be able to find out everything they need to know about your company from your website. When you leave consumers without any questions, you're clearing a path toward increased sales. I've already mentioned some information that every business should provide, but the following pages must also be part of your website:

- **"About" Page:** Every website should have an "About" page that tells customers who you are and what your company believes in. I see many websites with generic "About" pages—a single paragraph that doesn't say much about the company or its values. It's a lost opportunity to be transparent and build your customers' trust.

  Your "About" page should be one of the first pages in your menu. It should contain your mission statement and beliefs, and ensure customers that you value their experience and that you're dedicated to providing great customer service. Videos, pictures, or a letter from the owner can add validity and meaning to your "About" page.

- **"Team" Page:** The "Team" page is another opportunity to build trust through transparency. It familiarizes customers with your leadership and your employees. Sharing pictures, bios, and LinkedIn profiles puts faces to names, and puts your customers at ease.

  In my insurance business, I not only provide employee pictures, bios, and LinkedIn profiles on my "Team" page, I also have agents include their pictures and information in their e-mail correspondence with customers. So any time a customer is contacted by an agent, he or she knows exactly who the agent is, what the agent looks like, and how much experience the agent has. These details add a personal touch in an impersonal medium, resulting in high conversion rates and happy customers.

- **Pricing:** Be sure to include pricing on your website—especially if this practice is commonplace among your competitors. Listing the prices of goods or services shortens the sales process and builds customer confidence; they know exactly what they're getting and how much it will cost. If you don't list your pricing and customers have to call to find out, yet another step is added to the process, and every extra step can potentially impede a sale.

    I've seen many companies that do not list pricing on their websites because they charge different prices to customers depending on their means. If customers find out they are overpaying for a service, it could result in negative reviews and complaints against your company. Car dealerships create some of the most unpleasant buying experiences because of these murky pricing practices. It is so much easier and less stressful to be transparent. I always list packages and pricing, and include details about each one. By doing so, I answer questions before the customer has to ask.

These pages—in addition to your contact information—should be easily accessible and available in the main menu, the footer, or both. A clear and concise website with an abundance of content, resources, and external verification not only improves customer service, but also builds the transparency, trust, and loyalty required to secure a sale and keep buyers coming back.

Transparency—and Accountability—Start from the Top

Before the financial crash of 2008, Wall Street traders were making decisions about other people's money with little or no accountability. Because there were no repercussions, their choices became moral hazards. There were no consequences to their actions, they felt no obligation to their clients, and when the situation blew up, they weren't liable and did little to help. Moral hazards occur when there is no accountability. When clients complained about their broker, that feedback went into a black hole, never again to be heard—or addressed.

We've established that transparency is no longer optional—that you must provide your contact information, among other key pieces of data to prove your legitimacy. With transparency comes accountability; customers must know that if they need to reach you to return a product or get an answer, they can. They must understand their options for recourse, should they have a bad experience, and trust that their bad review or complaint will be heard, felt, and taken into account by the business. This level of accountability must also extend to your employees.

In order for transparency—and thus, accountability—to work, it must be a company-wide practice that begins at the top. From my experience, the number one way to ensure happy customers is to ensure that both your company and your employees are accountable.

In addition to knowing how best to reach the company if a problem should arise, customers must know that they have the power to address the experience they have with a specific employee. If they spoke to someone who didn't answer their questions, or, on the flipside, someone who was remarkably helpful and accommodating, there should be a route to review that employee. In turn, employees must understand that their behavior is not only a reflection of the company but also that it will have personal consequences or rewards.

The Takeaways

Transparency is a priority for every client and customer and is a crucial quality for any legitimate business. It is your responsibility to assure potential customers that your company is worth their trust, and that you will keep their information safe and secure.

The more information you can provide about your business, your employees, your policies, and your pricing, the more likely you are to make a sale. Business owners might not want to put themselves out there for fear of being scammed, but when you put yourself at risk, you prove your accountability, and reap the benefits. Put your name and contact information out there. Demonstrate how you do business. Your reputation is the most important thing you have, and it's always on the line.

My friend Rand Fishkin, who owns Moz, one of the world's biggest SEO firms, provides an astonishing amount of information about his company online. He lists every employee, all of his financials, and his personal information. He considers his transparency one of the main reasons for his success. His most valuable piece of advice? "You must be more transparent than your competition."

Questions for Consideration

1. What type of information do you want to include on your website's pages that can help increase transparency?
2. Which transparency tactics do you consider most important for your business?
3. How can you incorporate a contest, like the one described in this chapter, to help create trust between you and your consumers?

Visit **brianjgreenberg.com** *to receive additional free tips, as well as more detailed information on recommended services and strategies.*

CHAPTER 7

TWO GOLDEN RULES

I've always loved a good McDonald's breakfast. There's just something about an Egg McMuffin® and a perfectly crisp slab of hash browns that makes my day exponentially better. I'm not alone. For decades, millions of people rushed to McDonald's to get those Egg McMuffins and were out of luck when they arrived at 10:31 a.m.; at McDonald's, breakfast ended promptly at 10:30. Finally, in 2015, McDonald's heeded years of customer requests and rolled out longer breakfast hours. The addition was a huge success; customers came in droves. All. Day. Long.

While a customer-focused business is a fairly modern concept (which perhaps explains McDonald's decades-long hesitation), it is rooted in an adage as old as time, the Golden Rule: "Do unto others as you would have them do unto you." Parents, teachers, and just about anyone whose day-to-day life hinges on working with others has spouted this advice. It's so common because it's effective. In much the same vein, the golden rule of business is "Treat your customers with the same quality of service that you would like to receive."

My first forays into customer-centric business occurred when I was still a student in the University of Arizona's McGuire Entrepreneurship Program. Today, as a marketer and business owner with years of experience under my belt, I know the extraordinary value of a strong customer focus.

Rule 1: Treat your customers with the same quality of service that you would like to receive.

Reversing the Pyramid: What a Customer-Focused Company Looks Like

The old-school structure of business culture looked like a pyramid, with top management at the pinnacle, followed by middle management, frontline workers, and last—and often least—customers. But in the last several years, we've seen major shifts in the business community. Companies are now going out of their way to offer premier customer service, even when it negatively affects their bottom line, because they recognize that a customer-focused strategy often delivers long-term results. Today, customers sit at the top.

You probably experience this fundamental difference in your everyday interactions with businesses. Think back to the last time you called an Internet provider or credit card company. Who did you talk to, and where do you think that representative was located? For years, companies were outsourcing customer service to employees overseas. They made a move to save money, but it ended up really irking consumers. Now, many have learned from their mistake, and have set up their call centers back here in the U.S. It may cost a little more, but it certainly pays off.

Customer Service and Revenue: An Inextricable Link

When businesses don't care about how to best serve their customers, their revenue inevitably suffers. Dell is a perfect example. Initially, Dell made a name for itself by selling directly to consumers. Many companies—including my own—bought Dell computers exclusively and developed close relationships with particular service reps at the company. If we had any issues, we knew whom to call. But once founder Michael Dell took the company public and stepped down as CEO, the company made decisions that hurt its business big time. To increase profits, it started selling its products to big-box stores and outsourcing all of its customer service. Suddenly, we were dealing with anonymous voices overseas, rather than the reps we had come to know and trust. Dell ended up losing market share in addition to a ton of revenue.

Starbucks experienced similar circumstances when founder Howard Schultz stepped down as CEO. Howard was highly concerned with maintaining a strong client focus, and providing a consistent atmosphere. For instance, when Starbucks began serving breakfast sandwiches, everything began to smell like ham and cheese. Howard didn't like the fact that stores didn't have the same coffee scent that customers had grown to expect, so he invested money in developing ways to cook breakfast sandwiches without the stench.

After he left, the company started neglecting Howard's vision and the Starbucks customer experience. The new leadership stopped providing a homogeneous environment, without realizing that this is what customers had come to expect. As a result, Starbucks lost a lot of market share to The Coffee Bean, Peet's, and other chains that had picked up on the founder's brilliant insight and had begun selling a better experience. Howard Schultz decided to return and restore what he had created, and the company bounced back.

In the age of the Internet, the stakes are even higher now; news of your business's failure to serve a customer spreads much faster than it would have twenty years ago. In the past, the biggest risk was getting sued, which was a slow and expensive process. Now, just one bad review can have an immediate and detrimental impact on your business.

The Practice of Putting Customers First

Amazon understands how to put customers first. The company's CEO, Jeff Bezos, purposely leaves one seat open at his conference table during meetings. He says it's occupied by the most important person in the room: the customer. His approach is obviously successful; Amazon has been rated number one in customer service for many years, and the company's customer-centric approach is one of the main reasons it continues to grow.

Amazon takes plenty of losses. I've owned several Amazon Fire TVs and have had to call their service department because a remote stopped working. The first time it happened, they immediately shipped me a new remote and credited my account $10 to buy batteries. The second time it happened, they went ahead and credited my account $30 to buy a new remote—no questions asked.

There's a lot to learn from Amazon's business model—namely, the importance of addressing problems right away, and taking it a step further by offering something for the customer's trouble even before being asked.

This level of service will keep customers coming back. Transferring service issues to other people and making the customer jump through hoops for a resolution pretty much guarantees that they won't want to work with you in the future.

Another company that consistently ranks as one of the most customer-centric companies is Nordstrom. They have committed to focusing on removing as many customer pain points as possible. Instead of imposing many company policies on how to handle service issues, Nordstrom's employee handbook has only one rule: "Use good judgment in all situations."

This policy has led to some amazing customer-service stories including an incident in which an employee accepted a return for snow tires, even though Nordstrom doesn't even sell snow tires. Another story that resonates with me is about how employees will gift wrap products bought at other stores.

Nordstrom's service policy has resulted in the company outperforming its competitors,[10] even when all others in the industry are finding it difficult to grow their top line.[11]

Another example of putting customers first can be found at Marriott International. Marriott expects each employee to take a customer-centric approach, from housekeepers who check to make sure the alarm is not set before they leave a clean room, to employees in the social-media division who take pride in thoughtfully responding to customer tweets in real time.

Follow Through and Follow Up

While it's great to make promises to keep customers happy, it is imperative to follow through. It's not good enough just to ask questions, you must listen to the answers. After a while, you'll be able to anticipate customer interests and concerns—and most importantly, you'll be able to address them.

---

10 Gregory Ciotti, "How the World's Best Companies Focus on Their Customers," Help Scout Inc. May 9, 2016, https://www.helpscout.net/blog/customer-focus/.

11 Walter Loeb, "Nordstrom's Results Sat Its Strategy Is Spot On," Forbes, August 14, 2015, https://www.forbes.com/sites/walterloeb/2015/08/14/nordstroms-results-say-its-strategy-is-spot-on/#1b1f5c1b67e4.

For instance, my customers want tracking information so they can see when a product is shipped and when it will be delivered. When I tell someone he or she can expect to receive that information in an e-mail, I make sure to send it as soon as possible.

You can improve your responsive processes even further by utilizing technology to make sure your carefully derived business practices deliver every time. I now provide customers with automated tracking information, thereby eliminating about 40 percent of the customer-service calls my e-commerce companies receive.

Let's say you've made a sale and followed through on your customer's expectations. There's one last step: You need to follow up to ensure that your customer was satisfied and hasn't been left with any questions. In my businesses, we always contact customers after they've made a purchase. We thank them, send feedback forms, and provide discounts for their loyalty. Overwhelmingly, people are impressed that we took the time to ask about their experience. And we're happy to find out how we can improve our process and what we can do to address any concerns that might arise in the future.

Often companies will bust their butts to acquire a customer but won't nurture the relationship. There's a lifetime value to happy customers, and you should never waste an opportunity to satisfy them.

Rule 2: Happy employees mean happy customers.
The Value of Happy Employees

Customer focus may be the name of the game, but it's not achievable without buy-in from your employees. How do you get that? Focus on making *them* happy too.

Your employees are your direct connection to your customers. If they're unhappy, they won't show genuine enthusiasm or interest in promoting your product. That's going to come through, and it's going to impact sales. Maybe you've heard the saying, "Happy wife, happy life." In business, the phrase is, "Happy employees, happy customers."

If you take the time to ask your employees what hurdles they face on a daily basis, you will learn from them. And they will appreciate knowing that you value their insights and want to make their lives easier. In addition, having the inside scoop will help you make the sales process more efficient for everyone involved.

Of course, the first step is to make sure to hire the right people. In an interview, Howard Schultz, the CEO of Starbucks, was asked, "Howard, how do you get your employees to smile all the time? They're always so happy and in such a good mood." Howard responded, "It's easy. We just hire people who smile all the time."[12]

Communication Is Key

It is very important for employers to provide clear lines of communication for their staff. This is especially essential for businesses like mine that employ remote workers. My employees are all over the country. Some of them I've never met in person, even though we've maintained great working relationships for ten years or more.

I'll never forget a piece of advice from the book *The One Minute Manager* by Kenneth Blanchard and Spencer Johnson.

---

12   Howard Schultz, *Onward: How Starbucks Fought for Its Life without Losing Its Soul* (New York: Rodale, 2012).

They said that the most important thing a manager can do is hold a weekly meeting—even if it's virtual—in which each team member discusses what he or she did that week and what he or she plans to do the following week. We use RingCentral Meetings™ to conduct our weekly meetings, and those who are not in the office use their webcams so everyone can see one another. The service comes free with our RingCentral phone service, and you can pay for the same service at zoom.us. While we never want to bog people down with meetings, a weekly opportunity to touch base promotes consistency and accountability, and it helps people connect to one another and to the organization itself.

To further foster accountability and a sense of connectedness, employees should be able to communicate easily with each other. Providing an "intranet" for internal communications is an excellent practice. An intranet, not to be confused with the Internet, is a website accessible only to your internal organization. There are a variety of software programs available and methods of implementing an intranet to help employees engage with one another. For example, I use Woffice Premium WordPress Theme for my company's intranet. When Google got its start, it posted pictures of every employee on their intranet. That had the unexpected side effect of serving as an internal dating site. That's one way to build community!

In recent years, we've seen an influx of new tools that make virtual communication very easy. I use an instant-messaging system called Slack. Slack allows people to communicate with everyone on the team instantaneously. If someone is unavailable, the message is delivered via e-mail. HipChat, Zendesk, and Glip provide similar services to help cultivate employee communication.

Consider enhancing the impact of your intranet by encouraging employees to participate in surveys that bring to light their needs and insights. Employees can propose a project, and others can vote on it through the intranet. Such a program helps to build teamwork while unearthing exciting innovations.

Praise and Accountability

While it's obvious that everyone enjoys praise, honing employee accountability is just as important. People want to know that their contributions matter. With that goal in mind, I use a system called Objectives and Key Results (OKR)—the same system used by Google. Every quarter, employees meet with their supervisors and list two to five goals they hope to accomplish over the next three months. Each employee agrees to the set goals, and accountability is created.

I recommend holding meetings to discuss OKR every quarter, which is just long enough for employees to make headway on larger projects.

Remember, this process is not about micromanaging. Instead, it's a chance to tell employees when they're doing a good job and ask them for feedback on their own progress, combining praise and accountability to increase individual—and consequently organizational—success.

You can expand on the principles of OKR and promote transparency by sharing company objectives and key results at your quarterly meetings. Presenting valuable data, such as how many new customers you've gained or how many orders you've logged, paints a picture that reflects your company's health, demonstrates your own accountability, and offers an opportunity to enjoy some praise, as well.

Employee Empowerment

We've touched on the value of employee empowerment in terms of communication, accountability, and innovation, but there is no limit to the positive effects employee empowerment can have on your business: new ideas, new projects, even the freedom to make new (and valuable) mistakes. It's not just employees and customers who benefit from this kind of culture; you benefit as well, because it takes unnecessary work off your plate.

I like my employees to be able to solve problems as quickly as possible. To facilitate that, I give them the authority to incur a company loss of up to $500 in order to resolve a service issue. That means if a customer is upset, an employee can offer a refund of $500 or less without even asking me. The result is fewer headaches for me, and far better results for employees and customers alike. Everybody wins.

You can set whatever ceiling makes sense for your particular company; the point is that employees can make their own decisions with the universal goal of creating happy customers. When you empower employees, you have to accept that sometimes they might make the wrong decision. Maybe they'll give too much away. Maybe they won't give enough. Either way, it's bound to be a good learning experience for the employees involved.

Disempowering employees is as devastating to your bottom line as empowering them is beneficial. You never want to have employees who are frustrated because they don't believe that the company is going in the right direction and they feel like they can't do anything to change it. They will either bring down other staff and customers, or leave.

Organizations with empowered workers see lower employee turnover. This has both direct and indirect benefits. For one, you'll spend less time and money training new people. In addition, employees who stay on long enough to become well-seasoned veterans are better at enacting your vision. They'll build relationships with customers and do their best to anticipate customers' needs.

A vital aspect of employee retention is a living wage and competitive benefits. It's hard to put on a smile if you can't afford to pay your bills. Costco offers much higher salaries and better benefits than its competitors do.[13] So does Starbucks. As a result, employees at both companies stay longer and are more committed to promoting the company brand.

The Takeaways

To simplify the steps necessary to make your customers and employees happy, I've compiled eight simple strategies. They should come from the top down, and should be communicated to everyone involved in your business.

1. **Create an easy-to-remember company mission or philosophy.** At True Blue Life Insurance, instead of the sales rule "ABC," or "always be closing," we are committed to "ABN" or "Always be nice." After every meeting, I remind everyone to ABN. Always be nice to every customer, no matter what.

2. **Make your ethics visible to all.** It's important to make your ethics public via a page on your website or a sign on your wall. Make sure your ethics answer the most important question of all: Will they allow you to serve more customers?

---

13 http://money.cnn.com/2013/08/06/news/economy/costco-fast-food-strikes/

3. **Invest in a phone system that doesn't breed frustration.**
   People hate calling a company with an automated phone system and a maze of prompts. Instead, invest in an answering or receptionist service; it's less expensive than hiring a new dedicated employee, and the frustration you'll avoid will be priceless. For my True Blue insurance business, we use Ruby Receptionists, which has been a big hit among our customers and employees.

4. **Do not outsource your customer service or marketing.**
   You never want your customers to have direct contact with outsourced workers. Trust me. Your customers will always be able to tell, and it's just not worth their disappointment. Outsourced workers will never know your brand as well as a team of dedicated employees.

5. **Be willing to take a loss for your customers' sake.** Taking a loss on some business in a customer-focused model is not ideal, but your willingness to accommodate forms the basis of your reputation, a priceless asset. I encourage you never to be penny-wise and dollar-foolish in your customer-service policies.

6. **In a customer-driven business, there is no black and white.** There is only gray. Companies should address each situation individually. Committing to policies with no room for input or adjustment doesn't allow employees to make decisions necessary for success. As Ralph Waldo Emerson said, "A foolish consistency is the hobgoblin of little minds." One of my biggest pet peeves is when a company rep says, "If I do this for you, I'll have to do this for everyone." Policies

are never perfect; they are created by human beings. It's crucial to allow room for change.

7. **Solve issues right away.** Angry customers can ruin a business. In the age of Internet reviews, letting a complaint go unanswered can do immediate—and permanent—damage.

8. **Return messages promptly.** Whether it's a phone call or an e-mail, return all messages as soon as you can. In the age of smartphones, there's no excuse not to reply to an inquiry immediately.

Questions for Consideration

1. What are some ideas for your brand's philosophy?
2. What are some policies you can apply to your business to keep your customers and employees happy?
3. How will you allow your employees to give feedback on certain aspects of your company? Allowing employees to provide suggestions on how things can be improved is important: it not only helps your business but also tells your employees their opinions are valued.
4. How will you make sure your company's core values will not deteriorate after a change in leadership?

CHAPTER 8

THE THEORY OF RECIPROCITY

The theory of reciprocity is a key tenet of social psychology. It states that people are inclined to repay in kind what another person has provided. Like Newton's third law, in the realm of human interaction, every action has an equal and opposite reaction. Simply put, people tend to return favors. Marketing strategies capitalize on this impulse all the time; the world is full of free samples. But nothing's really free, is it?

For ages, sales reps have been treating people to lunch, dinner, or golf. The idea is that once your belly is full, you've finished your glass of wine, or you've made your last putt, you feel indebted. Car dealerships offer you a cold drink when you sit down. Banks provide free pens, coffee, or candy while you wait to talk to a representative.

You may feel slightly wary about accepting these tokens, and your instincts are right: Any gift, no matter how small, invokes the theory of reciprocity. Whether or not you realize it in the moment, you're being buttered up for a sale. Worse, even if you know on some level that it's a trick, it still works.

What's more, the theory of reciprocity works *even when you don't take what is being offered.* Here's a perfect example: At my local supermarket on Sundays, when the traffic is highest, there's always a sample table laid out with cubes of cheese, miniature cups of coffee, or tiny meatballs. When an enthusiastic employee offers me a meatball, he spends the time and effort to describe the company that produces them, the secret family recipe, and the array of meal options that these special meatballs provide. Even when I don't take it, his offer—of both information and the product itself—creates a sense of reciprocity between us. And if I do take the meatball and enjoy it, my desire to buy them is even stronger.

As a young boy, I watched my father's insurance agent, Bill Balkin, use the theory of reciprocity to charm his way through every door on which he set his sights. His methods worked on everyone from low-level administrators to Chicago's biggest celebrities.

Bill could have been a character in a classic movie. Though he must have been in his late seventies when I met him, he still had a youthful demeanor. He always, *always* brought gifts: an array of perfume samples and Bazooka bubble gum.

When he arrived at an office, he'd immediately give something away. As he approached a pool of secretaries, he would spread the perfume samples across a desk and let the women take their pick. He'd toss wrapped rectangles of bubble gum into the open palms of executives. Everyone loved Bill, and his great personality made him a multimillionaire.

Later on, I realized he was constantly invoking the theory of reciprocity. He gave people something that made them smile before making his sales pitch, and in turn, everybody he crossed paths with was happy to give him a moment of their time.

Applying the Theory

When I was in college in the early 1990s, I got a job with a company called Student Advantage. Student Advantage provided college kids with access to special discounts and information. The company was well funded, and it hired students at over fifty colleges to represent the new business.

Our job was to sign people up for the Student Advantage website. In return, we received four dollars for each student we registered. In addition to paying per individual, the company held a contest to reward the representative who got the most names.

I wanted to win. But nobody wanted to stop and listen to me talk about the nebulous benefits of this website. To make matters worse, when someone did stick around, the primitive touchscreen apparatus the company gave us to use for collecting information was slow, and the interface was hard to see in the sun's glare.

I realized I needed a new approach, and took it upon myself to print out the applications. But how would I get people to stop? I thought back to Bill Balkin and his briefcase full of gifts. His customers loved candy, and I knew college kids were no different. Armed with twenty bags of Blow Pops—the Bazooka of the 1990s—I proceeded to break all of my college's rules, driving my SUV into the center of campus and setting up a table right in the middle of the busiest pathway.

I passed out Blow Pops to anyone walking by. When they stopped to thank me, I asked them to take just a moment to sign up for Student Advantage. By and large, they were more than happy to reciprocate. Before I knew it, I was throwing Blow Pops across the street. People barely realized what had hit them before they were giving me their names.

Within two and a half months, I had registered more than four thousand people, blowing my competition out of the water. I had so many names that I had to hire a temp to help me enter all of the contact information into the company's website. I was only a sophomore, but I became Student Advantage's number one sales rep, all thanks to Bill Balkin's example and the reciprocity principle.

To this day, the theory of reciprocity continues to successfully fuel all of my businesses. I always provide something—a phone consultation, a coupon, a free quote—before asking for something in return, and it works.

How to Get Others to Help You

I learned a great lesson from *Never Eat Alone* by Keith Ferrazzi, a book I have already mentioned. The book's primary concept is that nobody makes it alone in this world; the totally self-made man is a myth. All successful people have received help from the people they meet along the way. Ferrazzi explains how to build and leverage these crucial relationships. He says that *the best way to get others to help you is to offer your help first.*

Considering this invaluable tip brought me back to a time when I failed to use the theory of reciprocity, a moment that's haunted me ever since. One of my first jobs after college was selling phone and Internet lines for a company called NextLink. I was sent all over Phoenix, Scottsdale, and the surrounding areas to sell new phone service and Internet-connection lines door-to-door and business-to-business. It was hard to get people to buy—especially door-to-door—so I went in to ask my sales manager for help. I'd seen Dean in action, and he was incredible.

"Sit down," he said as I walked through his door. He looked me in the eye and slid a $20 bill across his desk. "Get me to give you this $20 bill."

At the time, I was totally perplexed. I smiled at him and attempted to look casual. "Hey, can I please have that $20 bill?"

"No, you can't have it. Try again," he said.

"Look, I really need that $20. I need to pay my rent. I want to buy lunch today . . . "

He shook his head. I had no idea where he wanted me to go next. So, I got up quietly and left, feeling more than a little defeated. Shortly after, I quit. But for years, Dean's question bugged me. What would've been the right approach?

If I had to do it over again today, I would follow the lead of Keith Ferrazzi, Bill Balkin, and a host of successful salesmen before them: I would invoke the theory of reciprocity. I would offer to help him first.

I could provide him with a new idea to improve sales. If he appreciated my vision, he might be more likely to offer me that $20. I'd tell him we could consider it the start-up money to make it happen.

Or, I might leave the room and return with a fresh cup of coffee prepared just the way he likes it and say, "Dean, I want you to have this cup of coffee, and I want you to know that I'm very appreciative of everything you've done for me. You're a great salesperson, one of the best I've ever seen." Not only would I be giving him some much-needed caffeine, but I'd also be offering him a compliment—an additional gift. I would then follow up with, "Dean, let me know what I can do to help the company. Do you need me to knock on more doors?" adding Ferrazzi's approach into the mix. If he said yes, I'd say, "I'm on it. Could you lend me $20 for gas?" And he would probably say yes.

Now, I still don't know what my old sales manager was thinking. I can't go back in time. But I do know that I would have had a much better chance of getting that $20 bill if I had offered him something first and demonstrated my investment in our relationship. Always offer something first—your help, your time, or a small token that shows you are listening to your clients' needs and that you care enough to address them. I guarantee they will be more willing to return the favor and hear you out.

Share Something Small

Reciprocity is an important concept to understand and a valuable tool for customer buy-in. Offering something for free sets you apart from your competitors who aren't doing so. As businesspeople, we're trying to tip the scale in our favor. How are you going to get customers to stay on your website? How are you going to get buyers to share their e-mail addresses? Give them something!

Like many others, you might be worried about just giving something away, and rightfully so; anything that you offer is an investment, and it's hard to know how well it will pay off. *But it doesn't have to be something big.* Whether it's a stick of gum or a free pack of paper, you'll see that your small contribution has the power to ingratiate potential customers and ignite the sales process. Here are a few ideas for effective gifts that come at little or no cost:

- **Give Information:** One of the easiest things you can provide for free is information. Many websites will offer a free book download, television episode, or product sample before asking you to buy.

In one of my businesses, True Blue Life Insurance, I tried something unique. Everybody in my industry provides life insurance quotes online. People can go to my competitors' websites and receive personalized insurance quotes.

The catch is, the majority of my competitors require people to enter their contact information—their name, e-mail address, and phone number—before receiving their quotes. Nobody likes sharing personal information right off the bat. We all know that as soon as you type in your e-mail or phone number to access an article or video that claims to be free, you will start getting hassled by salespeople. And sometimes, this "free" information comes at an even higher cost, because one company will sell your information to eight others. Before you know it, your inbox is full, your phone is ringing off the hook, and you're well aware that whatever perk you received was certainly not worth the headache.

As a longtime disciple of the theory of reciprocity, I knew that in order to activate the power of this critical principal, the gift couldn't have any strings attached. I decided to set True Blue apart by making sure our quotes are actually free. People visiting my website can run all the numbers they want without entering a single piece of personal contact information. Not only do I provide them with quotes, but I also give them all the information I have: brochures of the companies they are considering, third-party ratings, and "Do I qualify?" questionnaires. I provide them with more information than any of my competitors. If they want to do their research before making a purchase, they can do it all on my site.

It costs me almost nothing, and the number of application requests I receive is ten times greater than that of any of my competitors. While 6 to 8 percent of visitors run a quote on my competitors' insurance sites, 60 percent of people run a quote on mine, because they don't have to share their information to do so. That means more people are entering my sales funnel, and the likelihood that people will call my toll-free number, hit my live-chat button, or fill out an application request is much, much greater.

Any professional offering a service, such as accountants, music teachers, and even marketers, can share information through free consultations. Even if customers decide that your services aren't the right fit for them, your efforts will create goodwill and reciprocity, as well as potential business down the line.

People are persuaded by those whom they like. Make yourself likeable, show a little kindness and consideration without asking for anything in return right away, and chances are, you'll grow your clientele.

- **Give a Free Trial or a Sample:** An opportunity to try your product or service for free can go a long way. A number of new online bedding companies—including Leesa, Casper, and Tuft & Needle—have disrupted the mattress industry by offering a quality product with easy shipping and terrific customer service. They also offer a risk-free trial period; potential customers can try their beds for one hundred days before officially purchasing.

  This works with smaller items as well. A free e-book, a meatball, a Blow Pop can all serve to get your prospective customers in the door, and even more successfully so if you don't ask for anything in return up front.

- **Give Out Smiles:** For years, I received calls from a man who sold promotional products, and every time, it was a similar pitch. "Brian, I'm Joe, with Empire Promotional Company. I want to talk to you about my business, but first I'd like to tell you a joke. Is that all right?" I told him he could.

  "A man in a diner says to his waiter, 'Excuse me; this coffee tastes like dirt.'

  The waiter responds, 'Of course it does, it's fresh ground.'"

  It wasn't the funniest joke I'd ever heard, but when he finished, I took the time to listen to his sales pitch, because he had made me smile. The theory of reciprocity can be as simple as a joke or an inspiring quote—any moment that improves someone's day makes you someone he'd like to listen to for just a little longer.

Investing in Reciprocity: How Much Is Too Much?

Figuring out just how much to give away is important. You want to make sure your costs don't outweigh the benefits. Every year, my janitorial supplies business sent out free catalogs to draw in new customers. They were beautiful and glossy, with an easy-to-read layout and clear contact information. But each catalog cost $12 to print and ship—a significant expense. On top of that, our distribution list wasn't tight enough, and we often sent them to people who couldn't bring in the revenue we needed to make it worth our investment. The same issues apply to any type of giveaway, even consultations, because your time has value too.

Do not give away anything that creates an undue burden on you or your staff.

The Takeaways

I'm not saying that giving people free soda at a car dealership will automatically get them to buy, but it could get them to sit down and listen. It might get them to take a business card or even test-drive a car, and move further along in the sales process.

Offer something small, without requiring anything first, and see how it works. A free consultation, a small gift, or even a joke might be all you need. Just make sure your investment is in line with your goals, and won't drain you of too many resources. Blow Pops won't break the bank.

Tailor your giveaways to fit your industry, take note of what others are doing, and set yourself apart. If you're offering the same coupons and discounts as everyone else, you won't stand out. Share something unique, even if it's as simple as a smile.

Giving stuff away makes you likeable, and likeability can have a significant impact. Bill Balkin's Bazooka gum didn't sell million-dollar insurance policies, but it probably got him the meetings.

Questions for Consideration

1. What types of benefits can your business offer in terms of reciprocity?
2. How can you implement reciprocity in your business so that your employees know it is expected?
3. What are some examples of reciprocity that you have experienced in your everyday life? Which were the most effective?

*Visit **brianjgreenberg.com** to receive additional free tips, as well as more detailed information on recommended services and strategies.*

SECTION IV

HOW TO KEEP GROWING

CHAPTER 9

WORK ON YOUR BUSINESS, NOT IN IT

I was fortunate to learn the wisdom of passive income as a kid. It all started with my grandfather, Sam.

After the war, with the encouragement of my grandmother, Sam decided to open his own business, a tavern in Chicago. Sam did well with the tavern, though he found himself working long hours, night after night. While sweeping up in the wee hours of the morning, he realized that the guy who provided the pool tables and jukeboxes for the tavern was raking in money while doing very little work. He would just come in once a week to retrieve all of the coins that the machines had collected. He had a system that was making money for him, when he wasn't even there.

A light bulb went off in Sam's head. He realized that the best kind of business is one that earns passive income and therefore doesn't depend on your time.

Sam decided to transition into the jukebox and coin-operated-games business and later sold the tavern. He had a friend in a county office who alerted him every time someone applied for a liquor license, which meant that a new restaurant or bar was opening in town. Sam would be the first guy at the new establishment, ready and eager to provide his jukebox services.

He was so good at it that he became known as "Sam the Jukebox Man of Chicago." He was that big.

Once Sam had built his business, he hired someone to collect the money for him. The operation no longer depended on him, and the money came flowing in. At that point, he had so much free time that he was able to start up some other businesses. He established a coffee business in which he would give out coffee machines to businesses and then just sell the coffee refills. He sent out coffee and received checks in the mail. Soon the only thing he had to do was go to his mailbox and collect checks. Sam retired at age fifty-five and enjoyed his leisurely retirement with my grandmother, Gertrude, in Florida.

My dad, Elliott, was next in line. After Elliott finished college, my grandfather got him a job at a company that manufactured video games such as PAC-MAN.

Once he'd learned about the industry, Elliott decided that he wanted to run a business of his own. He took out a line of credit and started going around to restaurants, clubs, hotels—anywhere he could think of—and selling them video game machines. He was great at making his sales pitch, including emphasizing that the restaurant would get a cut of the money the machines brought in.

Eventually, he did the same thing my grandfather did. He hired people to collect the money for him, and soon enough, he was making money while he slept. In all his free time he focused on expanding his business to cities all over the country. He would load fifty games onto the biggest U-Haul truck he could find and drive to a new city. Then he would drive around to bars, restaurants, and hotels, making his sales pitch until he had placed all of the machines. It usually only took him a couple of days, or a week at most. He would also have someone else with him as he did it. Along the way, he trained that person to become his money collector in that city.

He did that over and over again and before he knew it, he had routes all over the country, all running for him. Eventually, he decided to sell that business and start other businesses. He always followed the same pattern of creating something that would eventually run without him. To this day, my dad is still my mentor, and we still work together.

With my father and grandfather as role models, I knew from a young age that I wanted to own my own business. I already had the key to success: I knew I wanted to build a business that earned money whether I was there or not. So that's what I did. By the time I was twenty-seven, I was running my own businesses and earning passive income. Over the subsequent years, I've brought in more than $100 million in revenue. I earn money while I sleep.

If something happened and you were unable to make it to work, would your business still run? Would your doors still open? Would your bills and employees be paid on time? Would your customers' questions be answered? If you are such an integral part of your business's day-to-day operations that it cannot survive without you, your business is not sustainable. If you're too busy answering phones or cleaning the bathrooms or putting out fires to look at the big picture of your business and its future, you can't scale it or even think about selling it.

When you work *in* your business—moving from fire to fire—you can only focus on keeping things running. There's no room or time for growth. You end up chipping away at an endless to-do list of menial tasks, always busy, but never productive.

As a business owner or marketer, how you spend your time dictates what you'll accomplish. It's easy to fall into the habit of running your business instead of growing it, but if you want to increase your income, you need to increase the value of your time. Some call it building a growth engine; others call it growth hacking. The bottom line is that leveraging your employees, your website, and your marketing will save you time and allow you to focus on the big picture.

The Value Equation: Making Your Time Count

You can use a simple equation to determine the value of your day-to-day tasks and thus increase how much your time is worth. Using an eight-hour workday, when you calculate the hourly value of any particular task and multiply it by eight, you get the value per day. Maybe you don't work eight hours. Maybe you want to run the equation on five hours or four hours. That's fine. To determine the value of your time for the entire year, multiply that daily rate by 250, or the number of days you plan to work during the course of a year, and you'll get the annual value of the time you contribute to your business.

The goal is to give you an idea of how much bang you're getting for your buck. Let's say you're spending time doing the books for your business instead of growing it. That might be worth $35 an hour. If you're handling customer-service issues, your time might be worth about $20 an hour. Cleaning your office might be worth $12.

C-level tasks are worth considerably more. I'm talking about the kinds of activities that CEOs, CMOs, and COOs are doing. That dollar value per hour could then go up to $500 an hour or $1,000 an hour. These tasks can include creating processes for your teams to follow, hiring or recruiting top talent in your industry, forming partnerships within your field, finding investors, and promoting your business. The goal is to spend your time doing more valuable work.

Say that instead of spending the day answering calls—a $20-per-hour task—you're engaged in C-level tasks, worth about $500 an hour. If you multiply that hourly value by eight hours a day, that's $4,000 a day; $4,000 a day times 250 work days is about $1,000,000 per year, versus $160 a day and $40,000 a year for answering calls. If you want to earn a million dollars a year, you've got to spend your time doing tasks worth $500 an hour. Reflect on your day or your week. What did you spend your time doing? You don't want to be a foot soldier for your business; you want to be its general.

Maybe you want to get to the point where you are only doing C-level tasks, but you can't afford to hire someone to do the customer service or the accounting. The good news is, you don't need to. There are many different options today that allow you to either outsource certain tasks—like customer service—or automate them. You can easily use technology to become your best salesperson, without having to sell. More on that later.

Whether you have a staff of fifty or are a sole proprietor, when you enact a three-part system—delegation, automation, and systemization—the result is passive income and growth. You will see results if you implement even just one of these steps. If you implement all three, the possibilities are endless.

Delegation

Successfully owning a midsize business requires good delegation, the act of giving control, responsibilities, or jobs to others so that you can focus on the big picture. If you are still in the weeds of your company's day-to-day tasks, it's essential to transition from handling minutia to delegating it. When an owner has strong management skills and understands when to take on a project and when to delegate it—whether to an employee, an external company, or a software program—there's no limit to how much a business can grow or how successful it can become.

I understand that it's hard to give up control. But if growth is part of your plan, giving up control is inevitable. There are only so many hours in a day, and only so much one person can do. The more items you have on your to-do list, the less efficient you are at tackling all of them because your time and focus is diluted by the other responsibilities on your plate. If you're spending 40 percent of your day on accounting, that's 40 percent less time you have to focus on building your brand, crafting partnerships, or promoting your business.

We often create roadblocks to delegation. Maybe you think you can do it better than your best manager, because he or she is relatively new. Maybe you think no one will put the same care into handling your website development, your design, or your customer service because you're the one who built your company from scratch. Perhaps you're right. But to that I say, focus on **progress, not perfection because if you get caught up in making everything perfect, you'll never explore the limits of your potential.** Here are some time-tested tips to keep in mind when delegating to others:

- **Understand before you assign.**
  When I started each of my businesses, I did everything myself, from buying products to filling orders and addressing customer inquiries. While it is crucial to delegate effectively in order to progress, you must know the ins and outs of what you are assigning before you pass it on. Understanding each aspect of my businesses has allowed me unique insight into

not just how it should be done, but also how best to delegate it—and how to ensure that it is being done properly. If you don't understand a particular task associated with your business, you could easily be taken advantage of, especially when outsourcing. If you hire a contractor or a service to do a task you don't quite grasp, you can quickly lose control. You could end up overpaying, or worse. Plus, if your contractor is hit by a bus, you don't want to be out of business.

Even if you can't learn the job that you're delegating, make sure you at least understand it. Don't let anyone tell you something's too technical. If he can't put it into layman's terms, and express to you exactly what he's doing, don't hire him, because when it doesn't work out or takes twice the amount of time he promised, you won't have any recourse.

• **Be cautious about partnerships.**
Partnerships are very risky and seldom work. If your partner decides to stop doing his or her share, somebody else has to pick up the slack, and it's probably going to be you. However, as a part owner, he or she will continue to benefit from the business. In the past, I've made this mistake. I've partnered with engineers to start online businesses. When a particular project didn't work out, and my partner wasn't accountable, it was I who lost money.

I've learned that it works much better to hire contractors, especially contractors listed on freelancer sites that act as intermediaries. Such sites provide reviews for both freelancers and employers. They also provide guarantees; if the project isn't completed correctly, you don't pay.

I also suggest doing business with contractors who have a reputation to uphold. Consider hiring businesses with a presence on third-party websites like Yelp or Angie's List, because they are more likely to care about their reputation, and a bad review will make a difference to them.

- **Avoid paying hourly on projects.**
Keep in mind that when you are being charged hourly—rather than per project—there are many risks involved, especially if you don't understand exactly what a particular task entails. When a contractor or company is charging hourly, there is no incentive to finish on time, and when a project needs to be redone, you'll continue paying. In addition, if you hire people hourly, when they screw up, you have to pay them hourly to fix their mess as well. Try to get contractors to commit to a project price, so you don't end up paying more for their setbacks or mistakes. In addition, try not to pay up front to avoid lowering motivation. Once a contractor has his or her money, he or she may be less inclined to finish on time.

- **Use time tracking software for hourly remote workers.**
When outsourcing jobs to remote workers, I recommend using time tracking software that will take periodic screenshots of what they are working on.

    Some freelancers do not like the screenshot tracking for privacy reasons. I understand this argument, though the best remote workers won't have an issue.

    I use the time tracking software on upwork.com. I like it because it automatically pays the freelancer each week using my checking account.

    There are many software options for this. Do a Google search for "time tracking screen capture" to find free and paid services.

- **Make accountability non-negotiable.**

  In my businesses, we always request that customers leave feedback after any interaction with our websites or employees. I have also implemented call recording on my phone system to track customer service; it's often free with the purchase of an online phone system. Since employees know they are being recorded and that customers will be asked for feedback at the end of their call, they are often careful to provide high-quality service.

  Let employees and contractors know that their work will be evaluated, whether it's for customer satisfaction or the quality of their bookkeeping. Make sure that anyone you hire understands your goals and is willing to work to achieve them. For instance, consider hiring a salesperson on commission or requiring new employees to undergo a trial period to demonstrate that the quality of their work will dictate their level of success.

- **Set benchmarks.**

  Next, set benchmarks so that you can ensure that your business is operating on your terms, without having to do every task yourself. Contractors and employees alike should commit to and maintain your standards, and should provide their services within the timeframe you have agreed upon.

  Despite your best efforts, the work you delegate won't always come back exactly as you would like. But just because delegation doesn't work out every time doesn't mean you should give up on it. Consider the process of hiring a plumber. If you hire a plumber who doesn't fix your pipes correctly, are you going to give up on plumbers altogether? No, you'll just hire another plumber. The same goes for delegation: Don't give up on it just because it doesn't work out the first time. Evaluate your approach and try again.

Automation

At one point, my janitorial supply website featured 20,000 products. I wanted to be competitive and charge a little bit less than my peers, which required me to figure out what they were charging and make sure my items cost less. I could have asked an employee to go to each of my competitor's sites and see what they were charging for each product, and change my pricing accordingly—but that task would have been virtually impossible.

Instead, I chose automation. I hired a programmer to write a script that would scrape my competitors' websites for pricing information, which would then be logged in a database. At the end of the day, I had at my fingertips the names of five competitors, all of the products they sold, and what they charged for each one.

Next, I had my programmer write a randomization script that would price my product between one and nine cents less than that of the lowest competitor. That way, no one could say, "Hey, you're always two cents lower than me." There was no decipherable rhyme or reason behind my lower prices. For eight years, nobody could underprice me. As a result, my business saw amazing growth. It wouldn't have been possible without automation.

Technology provides innumerable opportunities for businesses; everything can be automated, from your books to your sales process. You have the option to use existing programs, which I'll describe in detail later on, or to build your own.

You might be surprised at how inexpensive it can be to build simple software to do simple tasks that will save you thousands of dollars. **The more you automate, the less you need to delegate.** You can eliminate the need for extra employees and allow your current staff members to spend their time focusing on meaningful tasks.

Employees can also provide a wealth of information and feedback on processes that could be easily automated. For example, my employees were getting hundreds of inquiries about shipment tracking, so I built a system to download all tracking information and send it to customers automatically. This simple task, which every major shipping company is already primed to do, eliminated 40 percent of our customer-service calls, freeing up hours of employee time.

By building in fail-safes, you can alleviate many of the concerns you might have about automating your tasks and systems. A website-monitoring tool can alert you to potential problems with your site. When building my site scraper, I included a fail-safe that prevented the program from selling my products below cost. That way, I could allow the automated system to do the work without worrying about losing money.

Systemization

McDonald's has thousands of restaurants that are essentially identical to one another, as do many other franchises. What makes McDonald's and every other franchise work is consistency, and consistency is the product of systematization.

Standardizing the procedures involved in running your business provides a framework that allows you to expand your operation. By creating processes that can be implemented throughout your company, you are improving time- and money-saving efficiencies while instituting best practices.

There is almost no limit to what can be systematized. Record the process for the next new hire and then create a training program for all employees. You could systematize your sales scripts, your return policies, the way you handle complaints, your representatives' uniforms, and the way your e-mails are organized.

It's also worthwhile to consider how you could increase the value of your business through tactics that don't require much extra work from you once you have a strong system in place. These passive-income generators will increase the value of your business, which is especially important if you plan to sell it. Whatever I do, I work as quickly as possible to systematize so that I can move on to growing yet another part of my business.

The Takeaways

If you feel as though you are constantly running around putting out fires and can't get to the work you really want (or need) to do, think about what you can delegate, automate, or systematize to clear part of your plate. In addition, consider how you can leverage your skills to generate passive income. You may want to offer a product and not a service, the sale of which can be easily automated and systematized.

I've learned how to delegate, automate, and systematize through trial and error. Now, if I want to take the day off, or if I'm sick, or if I want to go on vacation, my businesses still run smoothly.

It's imperative to build a system that functions without you because it's the only way to be scalable. Once you get to a point where you've freed up most of your time, you have some options. You can focus on the tasks you do best and enjoy the most or, with all that free time, you can start another business.

You *can* get there. You don't have to spend all day spinning your wheels. You can build your business so it runs without you, and I promise, it's the greatest feeling in the world.

Questions for Consideration

1. How valuable are your day-to-day activities of your business? How can you change the value of your activities to increase your profit?
2. How can you delegate, automate, and systemize to spend your time more effectively?
3. After you free up your time, what types of tasks do you want to focus on to improve your business?

CHAPTER 10

KEEP CUSTOMERS COMING BACK

When looking to grow your business, it's important to remember that while you're adding more customers, you must maintain the ones you already have. Any solid business plan needs to include some sort of resell, upsell, or cross-sell to keep people coming back.

Bringing customers back builds your clientele, saves you money and increases your sales. Why? It's far easier to increase sales from current customers than it is to acquire new ones. A Marketing Metrics study showed that the probability of selling to an existing customer is 60 to 70 percent, while the probability of selling to a new prospect is just 5 to 20 percent. For e-commerce sales, the latter is just 2 to 3 percent.[14]

Here are three reasons why repeat customers are often the best kind:

1. **Repeat customers spend more.** There are two factors to consider when thinking about the value of repeat customers.

---

14 Graham Charlton, "21 Ways Online Retailers Can Improve Customer Retention Rates," Econsultancy, July 3, 2015, https://econsultancy.com/blog/11051-21-ways-online-retailers-can-improve-customer-retention-rates/.

The first is how often they come back. The second is how much they spend per purchase. When customers have a good experience, they will not only come back more often, they will also spend more per purchase. Research suggests that a repeat customer spends 67 percent more than a new customer.[15] One reason is that they become aware of other services offered after spending time in a shop or on a site. Another reason is that customers who have already made a purchase tend to trust a company from which they've already purchased. Once you've proven yourself, you can get another sale that's equal or better, with less effort.

2. **Repeat customers save you money.** If you look at the statistics above, you'll see that it generally costs six to seven times more to acquire a new customer than it does to retain one. This alone demonstrates how much more profitable it is to expend energy getting customers to come back rather than solely on bringing in new customers.

3. **Repeat customers potentially make up the majority of business.** According to a study by BIA/Kelsey and Manta, small-business owners generate 50 percent of their revenue from repeat customers on average. For restaurants and salons, repeat customers make up more than 68 percent of sales. With at least half of the revenue coming from return

---

15 Jed Williams, "BIA/Kelsey and Manta Joint Report: SMBs Shift Priority to Customer Retention," BIA/Kelsey, April 3, 2014, http://blog.biakelsey.com/index.php/2014/04/03/biakelsey-and-manta-joint-report-smbs-shift-priority-to-customer-retention/.

business, you can't afford to skimp on marketing to current customers.[16]

The Second Sale

As you can see, turning first-time clients into loyal repeat customers has significant value. As such, the most important sale you'll ever make to a particular customer is the second one. Research suggests that a new customer has a 27 percent chance of purchasing again. But if that customer comes back a second time, the odds that she will make a third purchase jump to 45 percent. Each time she comes back, that number increases, making it easier and less expensive to encourage her return.

A study conducted by Bain & Company showed that increasing customer retention rates by just 5 percent increases profits by 25 to 95 percent.[17] Kissmetrics has shown that globally, the average value of a lost customer is $243.[18] If the potential additional profits don't sell you on the importance of customer retention, consider all the losses you avoid when you keep a buyer on board.

It's very important for any business to implement a strong plan to leverage its current customer base, even for professionals that seem to provide a one-time service, like real estate agents, insurance agents, and attorneys. Not only will clients possibly

---

16 Bizzy, "Love Thy Repeat Customers: They Are Your Most Valuable Customers," Bizzy, June 2, 2015, http://blog.bizzy.io/the-repeat-customer-is-a-treasure-trove/.

17 Frederick F. Reichheld, Phil Schefter, "The Economics of E-Loyalty," *Harvard Business School,* July 10, 2000, http://hbswk.hbs.edu/archive/1590.html.

18 "The Average Value of a Lost Customer is $243," New Media and Marketing, December 23, 2015, http://www.newmediaandmarketing.com/the-average-value-of-a-lost-customer-is-243/.

come back, but they might also refer the business to someone else.

The Importance of Keeping in Touch

In his book *Influence,* Robert B. Cialdini shares a wonderful story that continues to stick with me. Joe Girard is in the Guinness Book of World Records for being the greatest salesman of all time. In his 15-year career at a Chevrolet dealership in Detroit, he sold more than 13,000 vehicles, which comes out to an average of about five cars and trucks every day.

In 1973, at the peak of his career, Girard sold 1,425 cars, setting a record that may never be challenged, let alone broken. When reporters asked Joe how he managed to make so many sales, he offered just two explanations: a fair price and his likeable personality. That's it. According to his logic, all you need is a personable approach and a willingness to talk price.

What Joe didn't mention is how he stayed in touch with every customer. Joe knew that bringing his customers back was immensely valuable. In fact, every year he sent handwritten holiday cards to all of his customers, a task that became more difficult as his customer list grew to beyond 10,000. As a business owner, it's essential to get your customer's contact information. Joe's process must have been painstaking, but he knew it was worth the effort.

Think about every restaurant you visit, every haircut you get, every handyman that comes to your home. Are they taking down your e-mail, phone number, or maybe even your address? They should be.

You should think of each customer's contact information and e-mail address as little gold nuggets that you can cash in. After you get your customer's e-mail, you're in a position to leverage that gold.

Collecting Your Customers' Information

One of the most successful and cost-effective ways to communicate with your clients is through e-mail marketing. Sending targeted e-mails will help you spread your message and stay on their minds.

There are many different ways to ask for someone's e-mail address without being obtrusive. If you run a brick-and-mortar store, you can leave a sign-up sheet by the register. This may sound very old school, but it still works. While customers are checking out, ask them to sign up. I suggest telling them what they'll get if they do. For instance, if you plan on sending out coupons via e-mail, make sure you let them know what's in store for them. If you offer exclusive discounts, let them know.

One way of collecting your customers' information is through e-commerce software. With e-commerce software, contact information is easily integrated in your e-mail marketing software.

Now, you need a program that will catalog that information, so you can use it to stay in touch. The first step is choosing an e-mail–management software program. To find the right program for you, simply conduct a Google search for "e-mail marketing software." Some examples include: Constant Contact, MailChimp, ActiveCampaign, AWeber, Infusionsoft, and VerticalResponse. I've used every one of them, and currently use ActiveCampaign.

E-Newsletters

Newsletters are a terrific way to keep in touch with your contacts, and they provide the added bonus of building up a following that can be used as social proof. You can leverage your e-newsletter recipients to land a spot as a contributing author in publications such as *Forbes, The Huffington Post,* or *The Wall Street Journal.* These coveted news outlets value any traffic you can send them, because traffic translates into advertising dollars. If you are regularly communicating with 20,000 customers, that considerably raises your value as an author.

When is the best time to send your e-mail newsletter? E-mail marketing giant Constant Contact notes that while Tuesday and Thursday are traditional favorites, Monday has become the best day to get noticed. Most e-mail messages are sent between 10:00 a.m. and 2:00 p.m., so you want to avoid those times to prevent getting lost in the shuffle. Aim for either 8:00 to 10:00 a.m. or 4:00 to 6:00 p.m., and make sure to test the time's effectiveness using your e-mail marketing software, which tracks everything from opens to clicks.

E-mail marketing is much more effective than social media. Today, you can reach an average of 1 to 2 percent of your Facebook fans with each post, and an even smaller percentage of your Twitter following, but 79 percent of e-mail messages will make it through.[19] [20]

---

19   "Deliverability Benchmark Report: Analysis of Inbox Placement Rates in 2015," Return Path, October 2015, https://returnpath.com/wp-content/uploads/2015/10/2015-Deliverability-Benchmark-Report.pdf.

20   Erik Devaney, "Why Don't My Facebook Fans See My Posts? The Decline of Organic Facebook Reach," Hubspot, April 7, 2016, https://blog.hubspot.com/

For the last several years, e-mail marketing has been one of the most tried-and-true methods for cultivating new relationships with customers and strengthening existing ones. The flexibility of e-mail provides a wide range of benefits, including sharing the details of deals, news, and information while measuring the effectiveness of your campaign.

Loyalty Programs

Loyalty programs are one of my favorite methods for retaining valued customers. Everybody enjoys getting VIP treatment, and customers love to be rewarded for repeat business. It's a way of showing them that they're important to you. These programs are often built into e-commerce platforms already. If not, then you can usually purchase additional loyalty-program software. Just do a Google search for "loyalty-program software," and you'll inevitably find a good fit.

A well-developed loyalty program should be one of your major marketing initiatives. Consider the following options:

- **Points Programs:** Typically, loyalty programs use a simple points system. Customers earn points for coming back or buying more, which translates into rewards. Rewards can consist of discounts, freebies, or special treatment when a customer attains a certain amount of points; think cash back from your credit card or airline miles.

    It's crucial to make sure that people can easily use their points. If points are difficult to cash in, customers will feel worse than if there had never been a program to begin with.

---

marketing/facebook-declining-organic-reach#sm.00001sep6dir5e7vsmk2d6epw k6t6.

• **Tiered Systems:** Finding a balance between financially feasible and desirable rewards is a challenge for most companies when they design their loyalty programs. One way to combat this challenge is to implement a tiered system in which the more purchases a customer makes, the more rewards he or she earns. Start by offering small rewards, and encourage repeat customers to buy even more by increasing the value of the rewards as they move up the loyalty ladder.

I currently use a tiered loyalty system in my businesses. I've found it to be a great option not only to encourage repeat business, but also to reward my best and most loyal customers. I typically provide a 3 percent site-wide discount on the second purchase. By the time the customer places ten orders, he's reached the top of our loyalty ladder with a 5 percent lifetime discount.

• **VIP Benefits:** Consider charging an upfront fee for VIP benefits that enable customers to bypass common purchase barriers, a system that is actually quite beneficial for businesses and buyers alike. Offering a nominal upfront fee to get further discounts is definitely a good way to ensure that customers come back. One of the best examples of this right now is Amazon Prime, which charges an upfront fee of $99 in exchange for discounts on shipping, movies, television shows, and a whole slew of other services.

Amazon has incredible statistics showing how much its Prime members spend in comparison to non-Prime members. It's a wonderful way of getting customers to commit, but it is critical to ensure that you are offering sufficient value in order to get them to pay that upfront fee.

A VIP program is most applicable for businesses where a high volume of customers make frequent purchases. For an upfront fee, customers bypass the inconveniences that could impede future purchases—such as shipping or identity verification.

- **Games:** Encourage repeat shoppers by making a game out of the shopping experience. Take the McDonald's Monopoly game; every time you go to McDonald's, you earn game pieces, with the potential of winning big. I've fallen into the trap myself. I kept buying Big Macs to play that addictive game. But remember, some customers must win—the odds should be no lower than 25 percent—and the purchase requirements to play should be attainable.

When executed properly, these programs can work for almost any type of company, even a business-to-business seller.

Exclusive Discounts

Discounts and sales have been around forever. Why? Because they work. Coupons, sales, special offers, free shipping, storewide discounts, and special financing are all promotions that bring in repeat customers. A prime example of this is Bed Bath & Beyond's ubiquitous "20% off" coupon.

People argue about whether it hurts the company's overall profitability, but one thing that I know for sure is that those coupons get people into the store. If they just offered everyday low prices, I don't think they'd get the same amount of foot traffic. Coupons make customers feel like they're getting something special and increase the urgency of a purchase.

Direct mail is the most expensive strategy for distributing discounts. Besides being costly and time consuming to produce and send out, it's often thought of as "junk mail." I highly recommend e-mail when offering discounts. Let your customers print e-mails or scan them from their phone. Don't make promotions difficult. There's nothing more frustrating than being denied a discount that you expected to get.

There's nothing wrong with offering special incentives, but there is such a thing as too much of a good thing. Make sure to space out offers to avoid bombarding your customers. A great way of figuring out how often to send promotions is by analyzing your clicks and opens through your e-mail marketing software. You can even track the results of all your e-mail campaigns by installing a tracking code using your Google Analytics software. You can see how much revenue and how many orders your coupons produce. Set this up yourself, or post the project on Freelancer or Upwork. Plenty of professionals can help you install software to integrate your marketing campaign and your Google Analytics for a nominal fee.

The Takeaways

Repeat customers are where the money is, so it's essential to keep their attention and their business. Collect contact information and put it to good use with valuable incentives like loyalty programs, VIP treatment, and exclusive discounts. Your efforts will make customers feel the love and keep them coming back, putting more dollars in your pocket and less work on your shoulders.

Questions for Consideration

1. How will you keep customers coming back to your business?
2. Which tactics are most applicable to your business?
3. How will you gather customer's personal information without being obtrusive?

*Visit **brianjgreenberg.com** to receive additional free tips, as well as more detailed information on recommended services and strategies.*

CHAPTER 11

LET THE CUSTOMER TELL YOU WHAT TO DO NEXT

As business owners and marketers, we put significant time and energy into speculating about what our customers really want. Well, new technology and established techniques make it so you don't have to wonder anymore; all you have to do is ask. Your customers can provide terrific insight, and listening to them is a surefire way to ensure your business model is working best for both of you.

MIT's Eric von Hippel conducted a study that demonstrates how important customer input is to the success of any business.[21] He studied 1,193 commercially successful innovations across nine industries, and found that 737—or 60 percent—came from customer input.

He also found that the ideas that came from customers were far more profitable than the ones that came from companies. Internally generated innovations brought in an average revenue of $18 million, while user-generated improvements earned

---

21   Bill Lee, "The Things Customers Can Do Better Than You," *Harvard Business Review*, April 5, 2012, https://hbr.org/2012/04/five-things-customers-can-do-b.

approximately $146 million. Externally generated ideas brought in an astonishing eight times the value.

The largest and most successful companies in the world make it their practice to conduct polls and focus groups, especially when they're developing new products or services. Larger companies pay to hold in-person focus groups with their customers. While this might seem prohibitively expensive for smaller businesses with limited funds, new and affordable technology allows businesses to tap into their customers' minds without excessive costs.

To utilize your customers to their fullest potential, select any of the following techniques to gain insight on how to improve your business.

Paid Surveys

Online services enable businesses to issue paid surveys for much less money than physical meetings. You can even select participants that match your target demographic and income level. A simple survey can answer some valuable questions. You can ask customers if they'd be interested in a service you might provide, or share two different directions that you are considering and ask them which they'd prefer. Other issues to inquire about include your checkout process, customer service, and the sales experience.

These questions should be as simple as possible; most of the time, a series of multiple choice and yes/no options will garner the results you need. While some customers won't mind answering detailed questions, you may have to offer an incentive to get people to do much writing. Most online services carefully monitor the performance of the participants and grade their performance on surveys, so the quality of the feedback is far better than you might expect. A good place to find paid survey providers is on Google. Type "market research paid surveys" into the search bar to get started. Google itself offers a paid survey service at surveys.google.com. You can begin collecting feedback for as little as ten cents per survey.

Customer Feedback Questionnaires

It's always a great idea to send a short questionnaire after customers make a purchase. You want to find out what they liked and what they think you can improve on while the experience is still fresh in their minds. You could even offer a discount for filling out the form to increase the likelihood of their participation.

There are various survey tools that will host your questions, such as Pollfish, SurveyMonkey, Typeform, and Hively. Some larger companies use a service called Qualtrics. You can also use Google Forms to create a simple and easy-to-read questionnaire.

User-Experience Testing

Anything that happens to your customers when they're interacting with your business in person, on your website, or through an application process is part of the user experience, often abbreviated as UX. As an online business owner, I love user-experience testing services. They're inexpensive and incredibly insightful.

With UX programs, you can pay users to click through your website, and record their reactions. The software captures a video of their computer screen so you can listen and watch as they navigate your site. I used a service called UserTesting and got some excellent ideas from the feedback. Other companies that offer similar services are TryMyUI and UserBob. You can find a lot of these by searching for "usability testing."

When users navigate the site, they answer a set of predetermined questions. I can actually watch them as they provide me with commentary. Anytime they run into an issue, they'll mention it. You'll be amazed at how much you can learn from your customers' reactions. Many programs offer sample questions and templates as well.

The tests cost about $50 each—a worthwhile investment for the hour of feedback each paid user shares. Each user then receives a rating that indicates the quality of his or her feedback, ensuring accountability on both sides.

When testing the user experience on True Blue Life Insurance's website, we first provided a scenario for the potential customer:

> You're looking for life insurance for family protection, and conducting your research online. You're unsure whether you'll purchase from an online agency or brokerage firm, or go with a local agent once your research is complete.

Keeping this common scenario in mind helped users to evaluate the effectiveness of our website for our target demographic.

To shed light on the kind of data you can obtain from user experience testing, here is a list of questions we asked:

1. Look at the home page. Can you figure out what the company offers? Can you tell if it is better than its competitors?
2. Does this company seem trustworthy and reliable?
3. Think of something you want to find on this website and try to locate it.
4. Try to find a product that fits your needs.

5. After you find the product, quickly go through the process of buying it, without clicking the final "submit" button.

6. Imagine needing to research the company before committing. Search the Internet and see what you can learn about the company and its products. After completing your search, what is your impression?

7. If you wouldn't buy, sign up, or subscribe, please tell us why.

8. Based on what you've learned, do you think that people would be more likely to buy online, from a local agent, or call an insurance company to buy direct?

9. How might we convince people that we're the best option?

10. What did you like about the site? How likely would you be to recommend this site to a friend or colleague?

11. What frustrated you most about this website?

12. If you had a magic wand, how would you improve the site?

These questions offered a great deal of feedback about how our clients search for information and how we compared to other sites. Based on user responses, we made modifications to our website that specifically addressed why purchasing insurance from us was a better choice than purchasing directly from an insurance company or a local agent. After making the changes, we saw an increase in conversion rates on our website, which paid for the cost of conducting the surveys many times over.

Reviews

Throughout this book, I've discussed the importance of getting reviews. While positive reviews serve as vital social proof, negative reviews are extremely helpful in telling you how to improve. As you acquire reviews and feedback, take customers' concerns seriously. The most valuable feedback is often from someone who was unhappy with your product or service.

When an issue arises, fix it fast, and make sure it doesn't happen again. Then, take the time to call the customer and ask about his experience. Offer him something in return, like a refund or a credit toward his next purchase, to thank him for taking the time to speak with you. By implementing his suggestions or addressing his complaints, you can actually recoup the cost involved in making him happy, and potentially retain a buyer you would have otherwise lost to the competition.

Collecting Feedback and Suggestions

If you have a brick-and-mortar business, give customers the opportunity to comment on your service at the actual location. Try placing a suggestion box up front or give restaurant patrons the opportunity to rate their server when they receive their check.

Web-based businesses can put feedback widgets on their sites, giving customers a chance to report any issues. Search Google for "customer-feedback software" and you'll see many different software services that can collect this information. Some of them are Feedbackify!, GetFeedback, SimpleFeedback, Survicate, Usabilla, Client Heartbeat, and Hotjar.

Many of these widgets go beyond giving people the opportunity to make suggestions; they also offer some sort of poll or questionnaire right on your website. At a cost of $15 to $50 per month, it's an accessible tool with significant benefits.

Request Polling/Voting Software

Some of the best software companies offer customers the opportunity to vote on what they'd like to see companies develop next. UserVoice, The IdeaWall, and UseResponse are all feedback programs that can capture this information. Many companies will also use the same tools to get feedback from their employees. By polling, you can evaluate the market to determine how your idea will play out before you invest in it. Customers vote on the features that are most important to them, driving the most voted features to the top of the request list. Evernote is one example of a software company that encourages their users to vote on what features or fixes are performed next by the company.

Make sure that you're transparent about this process; let customers and users know what you're thinking and get their feedback. Some companies are hesitant to share information openly because they don't want their competitors to know what they might be working on next. But trust me when I tell you that fear will hinder your success. Transparency is something I promote throughout this book, and a tenet I insist on throughout each aspect of every business I own.

Employee Feedback

While it's essential to glean and analyze customer feedback, you can't underestimate the value of employee opinions. Since your employees work for the company, they have a lot at stake, and they can be an excellent resource for learning more about customers' interests as well. Frontline employees, who speak directly to customers, have great insight as to what customers are looking for. So make sure you ask your employees—especially those in sales and customer service—what ideas they have for improving the company and what direction you think you should take.

I frequently ask my employees what their calls are about, what questions they hear most often, and what complaints come in. If I can respond to the potential questions and objections customers may have right away—even before they have them—I can continue to sell without selling and spend the morning sleeping in. Using this method, I've been able to get customers through the entire buying process without even talking to them.

When employees know that the company is willing to take action, and that I am interested in handling customer service and sales issues without adding work to their plate, they're much happier and more likely to provide effective feedback. It's a win-win on every level. To incentivize even further, you can offer prizes for the best ideas on a quarterly or annual basis.

Competitive Analysis

One way to find out what your customers want is to look at what they're buying. I always encourage companies to keep an eye on what features and products their competitors are offering, and to watch for anything new happening in the marketplace. If you see a product or service popping up more frequently, it indicates that customers want it. If a competitor comes out with a new product, try some of the strategies mentioned in this chapter. Can a better version of a similar feature work for you? You won't lose customers to competitors if they know that you're going to continue to innovate and offer what they want. A successful business is an agile business.

The Takeaways

There are many ways to find out what your customers are seeking. Some methods require a small expenditure, but the input you'll get will be well worth it. Incorporate the feedback of both customers and employees into your plans to reap the benefits of their brilliant ideas and create a culture where everyone feels valued. When you implement the ideas and feedback of your target demographic and the people who assist them every day, you'll be on your way to increasing your effectiveness—and profitability.

Questions for Consideration

1. What feedback strategies would fit best for your company?
2. What types of products and services are your customers typically interested in? How can you leverage this information?
3. How can receiving consumer feedback build trust between you and your consumers?
4. Are there incentives you can offer customers to provide their feedback without costing your company much money?

CHAPTER 12

FINAL THOUGHTS

Armed with the strategies in this book, you are ready to become your own marketing guru and make your business the most successful it can be. One of my favorite quotes is from the movie *Tin Cup*. In the movie, Kevin Costner plays Roy "Tin Cup" McAvoy, an aging golf pro who qualifies for the US Open. Recalling his philosophy on why he chooses to accept challenges and go for it, Roy says, "When a defining moment comes along, you define the moment, or the moment defines you."

This is *your* moment. It's time to take action.

Many of these tools require a commitment of time, energy, and a little bit of money, but they will pay off. Using these tactics, I've been able to develop many systems that run on their own. Customers find me online and continue to make purchases every day. Orders come in very early in the morning and very late at night. They pour in while I'm working on other projects, and even while I'm on vacation with my family.

Effective marketing is like building up assets that produce dividends. Every time you contribute to your assets, you are building a foundation that will continue to bring in revenue for the long haul.

My father likes to say, "Work while you're young, and then you can relax." Whether you're young or old, if you put in the effort now, you can reap the benefits for years to come. You're casting a net on the Web that will continue to catch customers even as you move on to your next business endeavor.

It's essential to give your marketing plan your best effort and to understand each technique you employ. I hope that after reading this book, you will understand why you're using these strategies and be familiar with some of the new technologies that make them easier to put into practice. That way, you can choose the options that will work best for you.

So much of marketing is connecting all of your initiatives in order to best leverage your time and your outcomes.

You've heard the expression, "Kill two birds with one stone." Some of these techniques will allow you to kill six birds with one stone because there are direct and indirect benefits for each, and by now, you should have a feel for how these efforts interact and compound to deliver better results.

As you continue to build your business and encounter challenges and potential solutions, new questions might arise. What's the best review software? What's the best user-testing program? What's the best social-media platform? In each chapter, I've made recommendations for these products. But I encourage you to visit and use my website. It's a living tool, and is continuously updated as new information becomes available. My goal is to serve customers. As a reader of this book, you are my customer. I want to provide you with everything you need to create a passive sales system—a system that brings in customers 24/7, even as you sleep. I hope you'll stop by from time to time at brianjgreenberg.com. I want to continue to help you become a salesman who doesn't sell, even after you've finished this book. Together, we can create an enduring legacy for your business that works in perpetuity, so you don't have to.

Questions for Consideration

1. Currently, what are some of your company's best assets? After reading this book, what can you do to improve these assets?
2. How much time, energy, and money are you willing to put into your marketing strategy?
3. What does your business mean to you personally? How will you demonstrate this to both employees and customers?

Morgan James
Speakers Group

www.TheMorganJamesSpeakersGroup.com

We connect Morgan James published
authors with live and online events
and audiences who will benefit
from their expertise.

Printed in the USA
CPSIA information can be obtained
at www.ICGtesting.com
JSHW022345140824
68134JS00019B/1689